HIGH LATITUDE
SAILING

HIGH LATITUDE
SAILING

SELF-SUFFICIENT SAILING TECHNIQUES
FOR COLD WATERS AND WINTER SEASONS

JON AMTRUP & BOB SHEPTON

ADLARD COLES

LONDON · OXFORD · NEW YORK · NEW DELHI · SYDNEY

ADLARD COLES
Bloomsbury Publishing Plc
50 Bedford Square, London, WC1B 3DP, UK

BLOOMSBURY, ADLARD COLES and the Adlard Coles logo are trademarks
of Bloomsbury Publishing Plc

First published in Great Britain, 2020

A catalogue record for this book is available from the British Library
Library of Congress Cataloguing-in-Publication data has been applied for
ISBN: HB: 978-1-4729-7327-6;
ePDF: 978-1-4729-7325-2;
eBook: 978-1-4729-7326-9

2 4 6 8 10 9 7 5 3 1

Typeset in Berling by carrdesignstudio.com

Printed and bound in China by Toppan Leefung Printing

To find out more about our authors and books visit www.bloomsbury.com
and sign up for our newsletters

The extract from *Nattåpent*, copyright © 1985 Ralf Jacobsen, was reprinted
with permission from Gyldendal Norsk Forlag

CONTENTS

Sea Ice Extent, September 2019, National
Snow and Ice Center, nsidc.org
(The Arctic ice will be closer to the shores
of Canada, Alaska and Russia in June)

*Bering
Sea*

Ayon

Providemiya

*East Siberian
Sea*

Nome

Cape Dezhnev

Bering Strait

**Wrangel
Island**

Point Hope

P A C I F I C

*Chukchi
Sea*

O C E A N

A L A S K A

(U.S.)

Point Barrow

Anchorage

A R O

Herschel Island

O C

Tuktoyaktuk

*Banks
Island*

McClure Strait

Queen Elizabeth Islands

Parry Islands

*Melville
Island*

Lancaster

**Ellesmere
Island**

C

*Victoria
Island*

*Bathurst
Island*

Nares Strait

Cambridge Bay

*Prince of
Wales
Island*

Resolute

*Devon
Island*

Qaanaac

*Tasmania
Islands*

Peel Sound

*Somerset
Island*

Dundas Harbour

*King
William
Island*

*Bellot
Strait*

Prince Regent Inlet

Arctic Bay

*Melvi
Bay*

Gjoahaven

Pond Inlet

Baffin Bay

Baffin Island

Upernav

*Foxe
Basin*

Clyde
River

*Dis
Isla*

Qeqertarsu

N

A

*Hudson
Bay*

D

A

Davis Strait

Manits

1000km

1000miles

· · · · · Northwest passage

· · · · · Northeast passage

140° **130°** **120°** **110°** **100°** **90°** **80°** **70°**

S i b e r i a

R U S S I A

S

Tikai

Laptev Sea

Novosibirsk Islands

North Land

Taimyr Island

Kara Sea

Cape Zhelaniya

Novaya Zemlya

Arkhangel'sk

60°

50°

40°

30°

20°

T I C

E A N

North Pole

Franz Josef Land

B a r e n t s S e a

Svalbard

Nordaustlandet

Verlegenhuken

Spitsbergen

Longyearbyen

85°

80°

Vardø

Murmansk

FINLAND

SWEDEN

G r e e n l a n d S e a

Tromsø

Bodø

NORWAY

Arendal

GREENLAND

(Denmark)

Jummaanaq

asiaat

Scoresbysund

N o r w e g i a n S e a

70°

Arctic Circle

Denmark Strait

Isafjördur

ICELAND

Olafsvik

Reykjavík

Keflavik

Vestmannaeyjar Island

Tasiliaq

North Sea

60°

uk

Paamiut

Qaqortoq

Cape Isolation

Prince Christian Sound

Cape Farewell

ATLANTIC

OCEAN

40° **30°** **20°** **10°** **0°** **50°** **10°**

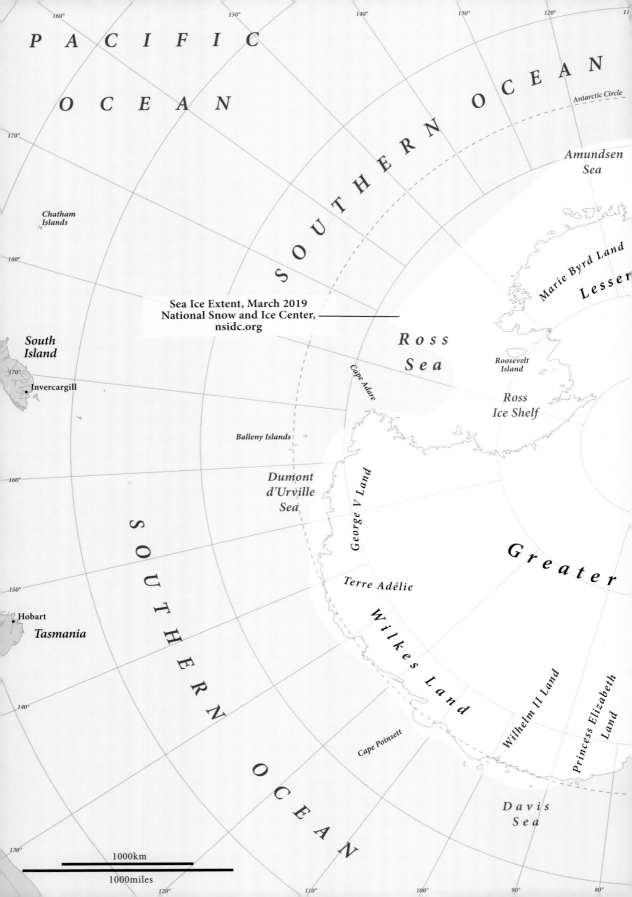

P A C I F I C

O C E A N

S O U T H E R N   O C E A N

Antarctic Circle

170°

180°

170°

160°

150°

140°

130°

120°

11

Amundsen
Sea

Marie Byrd Land

Lesser

Chatham
Islands

South
Island

Sea Ice Extent, March 2019
National Snow and Ice Center,
nsidc.org

Ross
Sea

Roosevelt
Island

Ross
Ice Shelf

Invercargill

170°

160°

150°

140°

130°

Cape Adare

Balleny Islands

Dumont
d'Urville
Sea

George V Land

Greater

S O U T H E R N

Terre Adélie

Wilkes Land

Wilhelm II Land

Princess Elizabeth
Land

Hobart

Tasmania

O C E A N

Cape Poinsett

Davis
Sea

1000km

1000miles

130°

120°

110°

100°

90°

80°

CHILE

Tierra del Fuego

Ushuaia

Cape Horn

Falkland Islands

Port Stanley

Drake Passage

Peter I Island

Bellingshausen Sea

Thurston Island

Sile land

Charcot Island

Adelaide Island

South Shetland Islands

Elephant Island

Clarence Island

Scotia Sea

Graham Land

Joinville Island

Ellsworth Land

Alexander Island

Antarctic Peninsula

Antarctica

South Orkney Islands

South Georgia

Ronne Ice Shelf

Weddell Sea

ATLANTIC OCEAN

Berkner Island

Coats Land

Cape Norvegia

South Pole

85°

80°

Antarctica

OCEAN

Dronning Maud Land

Mac. Robertson Land

Kemp Land

Enderby Land

70°

Antarctic Circle

60°

SOUTHERN OCEAN

50°

Cape Ann

ATLANTIC

Cape of Good Hope

Cape Town

1 INTRODUCTION

I could barely see the bow 43 feet away. The ski goggles took the pain away from my sore eyes. I was still captured in the white stuff. The snow was everywhere and so could other boats be. I couldn't see them, and they couldn't see me. I just had to accept the fact and be happy in the all-white world.

The one thing in my favour was that it was mid-February and I was sailing well above the Arctic Circle. I hadn't seen any other boats since I hoisted sails in the pitch-dark morning 12 hours ago.

As day broke, I sailed through a maze of low islands and skerries. The high-water mark was where the snow line ended. I was on a falling tide with following winds. All was in my favour, except for the fact that I was sailing south in the northern hemisphere.

To quote Rolf Jacobsen, one of Norway's most respected poets:

North is best.
The fiery winter sky, summer night sunshine miracle
Walk in to the wind. Climb mountains.
Look to the North.
More often.
This country is long.
Most of it is North.

I was running low on water. The fresh snow was very welcome in that respect. Owing to the cold, I had not been able to get any fresh water from taps on the docks. Everything was closed down and wouldn't open before winter retreated to the mountaintops. I had to melt snow. It just made the wilderness experience more intense, bordering on an expedition ambience. It was a truly different world.

ICE IS EVERYTHING

We live in a world where everything is just around the corner. Water on tap. Water in bottles with a thousand different tastes. It's so ordinary that not even the launch of yet another novelty bottled water makes you wonder when it will stop. Everything is available. All the time. You don't have to plan a single thing. Everything can be fixed by picking up the phone, or you can mail, chat, tweet, or google it.

When you sail in remote places like Svalbard, Greenland or South Georgia, you can't do that. You are on your own in all respects. You have to be totally self-sufficient and lay your plans accordingly. But when you have done that and acted on it, you are free, and satisfied. Free from everyday trivialities like bills, newspapers, crappy TV series, driving to the shop just to buy oregano, and all the other stuff that doesn't necessarily make you happy. Here, it's just you and nature, and it's up to you and your own competence.

▲ *Dodo's Delight* amongst the icebergs, West Greenland.

▲ Some ice floes are big enough to walk on, such as these in Tasmanian Islands, Northwest Passage.

Day in. Day out. All that changes is the scenery as new landscapes appear, and the wonderful feeling of remoteness.

The environmental aspect of a trip to the high latitudes is in itself worth the effort. As you plan the trip you will have to consider how to economise water, electricity, fuel and food. Resources may be scarce globally, and most certainly are on a trip in a boat with limited capabilities (and capacities). When you sail to the high latitudes, you are a small self-reliant community.

And when you are sailing, you have to manage the waste you produce. And it's a lot. It makes you think, and it makes you wonder where this is going. But most of all, it might change your habits when you get back to what is called real life.

GET OUT THERE

Twenty years from now you will be more disappointed by the things that you didn't do than by the ones you did do. So throw off the bowlines. Sail away from the safe harbour. Catch the trade winds in your sails. Explore. Dream. Discover.

H. Jackson Brown Jr.

Some prefer warm days, no rain and marinas with all the comforts within walking distance when they sail. Most people have a perfect life that way. Some of us, though, and I expect it will be more and more, believe that the more clothes you have to wear, the greater the experience. The goal on this vacation is not to get a tan. We want an adventure. We want to challenge ourselves. We want more out of life. The high latitudes are where you can still do some proper exploration. The rest of the world is more or less just well-established infrastructure by comparison.

We can accept the occasional gale just to experience something completely different. Dealing with the gale in itself becomes the icing on the cake, so to speak. And we are prepared for it. We have planned for it, and we can take it. Sailing in the high latitudes is all about how you adapt and learn. You have to calculate risk and improvise, because there is no definite answer to any question. That's when you get the exhilarating feeling of meeting the challenge.

Jon Amtrup

▼ Safely anchored in Stella Creek by the ex-BAS Faraday Base, Antarctica.

Such beautiful regions are just waiting
to be explored.

2

ABOUT THE AUTHORS

JON AMTRUP

Jon Amtrup has been sailing and writing for most of his life – and intends to continue. He has sailed the Norwegian coast summer and winter a number of times, crossed the Atlantic twice, circumnavigated Svalbard, sailed in Greenland, crossed the North Sea 13 times and competed in a number of double-handed and short-handed regattas, both national and international. He has also assisted several high latitude sailing expeditions with advice and weather and routing assistance, and delivered a number of yachts.

He studied political science, sociology and Eastern European studies at the University of Oslo, journalism in Bodø and PR and management at Norwegian Business School. He has worked as a journalist in newspapers and magazines in Norway, and as a freelancer contributing to SEILmagasinet and various international sailing magazines.

He is a member of The Explorers Club.

See www.explorenorth.no for more information and contact information. All feedback is very welcome.

◀◀ Even quite large ice floes can be moved away with a tuk (ice pole).

REVEREND BOB SHEPTON

Reverend Bob Shepton is a highly experienced Arctic explorer, who has led several sailing and climbing expeditions to Greenland and Arctic Canada in his yacht, the Westerly 33 sloop *Dodo's Delight*. He acts as Arctic advisor/ice pilot to sailing and climbing expeditions and undertakes yacht skippering. He has circumnavigated the world via Antarctica and Cape Horn, made 15 Atlantic crossings so far, and has traversed the Northwest Passage twice, east to west in 2012, and then west to east in 2013, in his own small boat. He 'happens to have sailed in every ocean of the world' and was elected British Yachtsman of the Year 2013. See www.bobshepton.co.uk for more information and how to get in contact.

TROND AASVOLL

Trond Aasvoll is an experienced short-handed sailor and explorer. In 2010, he and two fellow explorers set out on a circumnavigation of the North Pole. The plan was to do it in one season. It wasn't lack of grit or the ice that stopped them, but the Russian authorities. They finished their circumnavigation the year after and became the first Norwegians ever to transit both the Northeast Passage and Northwest Passage. Aasvoll is a highly sought-after skipper for Svalbard expeditions, and has also logged thousands of miles as skipper and short-handed sailor in regattas and cruising. He is a member of The Explorers Club.

ELENA SOLOVYEVA

Elena Solovyeva got involved in sailing as a hobby, but eventually it turned into her work and passion. Now a professional sailor, she knows how to make your voyage go smoothly. During her sailing career she has been chief mate on the yacht, *Peter I*, for its circumnavigation through the Northeast and Northwest Passages in 2011 and became the first and so far the only woman who has sailed around the North Pole in one season, and she is the first woman to have sailed both the Northeast and Northwest Passage in one season. She then became CEO of a yacht travel company and director of Adventure Race 80dg regatta.

▶ High and dry. A kick up keel has its benefits as you can beach the boat or anchor in very shallow water.

▶▶ *Dodo's Delight* creeping past an iceberg, West Greenland.

Dodo's Delight dwarfed by a huge iceberg, West Greenland.

3 PREPARING YOURSELF

STATE OF MIND

Sailing in the high latitudes requires experience, planning, stamina, guts and a special state of mind. As with most other things, you can train for a high latitude expedition. If you live in a country with a winter season – use it actively for cruising. Don't put your boat on the hard for the cold season. Spend the weekends and afternoons sailing so that you are prepared for the real thing. Start in the autumn. Anchor in small bays that are partially exposed to learn anchoring techniques and how to arrange lines ashore. Read the weather forecast thoroughly to avoid putting yourself in dangerous situations when training. When lines and anchor are set properly, you will be surprised how much wind and sea you can ride out. Be sure always to have an exit plan if things should turn out for the worst.

Exploring in remote areas is a challenging mind exercise. It's not just about keeping warm and alert. As you sail along a new coast where the weather can be highly unstable, you always need to have contingency plans.

▲ Having suitable clothing can be a great help.

◀◀ Every iceberg is different.

> *I may say that this is the greatest factor – the way in which the expedition is equipped – the way in which every difficulty is foreseen, and precautions taken for meeting or avoiding it. Victory awaits him who has everything in order – luck, people call it. Defeat is certain for him who has neglected to take the necessary precautions in time; this is called bad luck.*
>
> Roald Amundsen, *The South Pole*

Think worst-case scenarios for when sailing, before anchoring and after you have set your anchor. What if the wind shifts? Will the anchor hold? Will ice come drifting? Where can I escape to? Do I have enough room to manoeuvre?

Always have a back-up plan for the back-up plan. Self-sufficiency and being prepared for redundancy are the key in high latitudes. And to avoid problems it is important to have established routines that work:

Sailing and climbing go
so well together.

▲ Dodo's Delight wintering in Nome, Alaska, after the east-west transit of the Northwest Passage.

- Always have the boat ready for rough weather, both below and on deck. Make sure everything has its own place on board, and that everyone puts things back after use. This will give you the ability to hoist anchor immediately without a lot of things breaking or being thrown around down below.

- Establish routines on deck so that you sail with a clean deck. If you have to stow diesel cans, dinghy etc on deck, make sure they are always secured when not in use.

- Potential breakages or chafe or anything else that can become a problem must be fixed straight away. If your mindset is 'it can wait until tomorrow', then the problem might be a whole lot bigger and the weather much worse when it becomes essential to fix it. The moral is to fix things immediately. Always.

- Also establish routines when sailing into the night. It's a good habit to check all halyards and sheets before night falls. They must run free and not be tangled with other lines or the rig. Prepare the sails you expect to use during the night. If you are sailing along a coast, think about which anchorages or harbours you could go into along the way if the weather should turn bad, or the feeling of tiredness becomes too overwhelming.

- When starting the engine, always check for lines in the water before pushing the button. Then check that the cooling water is pumping out freely and no unusual sound is coming from the engine. Check the oil level every morning before heading out.

- You are probably doing these things already, but all this is routine that will heighten your awareness and most likely give you a trouble-free and happy expedition.

- Think comfort before speed. It is always better to wait a few hours, or even a day or two, instead of setting out into a nasty sea or bad weather prognosis. It is easier on the boat and crew. And to be perfectly honest, what does a day or two matter in the grand scheme of things? Take the time to enjoy yourself where you are, right now.

RISK ASSESSMENT

Sailing in high latitudes should be a continuous exercise in risk assessment. You are often far away from help, hospitals, medicine or transport other than your own vessel. That's why it is very important always to identify possible risks, together with possible solutions. You have to be more careful than usual as help can be very far away and even small injuries can be potentially lethal in the worst case, or at the very least put an end to the expedition.

▨ FAMILIARISATION WITH AREA

One of the many joys of going on an expedition is studying maps, books and videos or speaking to people who have been in the area before you. Gather as much knowledge and information as you possibly can, and be sure to write it down as your research progresses. Don't be scared to call or mail other explorers to get their take on the area and conditions. Most people like to share their knowledge and many are even honoured to be contacted and asked if they can share their experience.

Possible ports/refuges

Study a map or chart of all possible ports and safe anchorages along your planned route before you leave. Do the same exercise as you sail so you have at least a sketchy plan for where to head to if the weather turns bad, ice starts coming in, the engine fails or the crew are on the brink of exhaustion.

SAR facilities in the area

Solitude and the feeling of utter remoteness is one of many reasons why we sail to the high latitudes. You can only depend on yourself.

A few of the really hardcore high latitude sailors refuse to push the emergency button when things start to go bad. They have accepted that they are taking risks out of the ordinary and don't want to expose other people (aka rescuers) to the same risk just because they have done so. In most areas in the high latitudes a rescue mission is highly risky, and expensive, and what's even worse for the persons in peril is that the rescue can at best be days away. Sometimes weeks. Svalbard is the exception, as a rescue chopper out of Longyearbyen covers the whole area, weather permitting.

In the Northeast Passage you can expect not to be rescued at all, as the north coast of Russia has very few helicopters and rescue vessels stationed within reach. In the Northwest Passage the situation is somewhat better due to the Canadian Coast Guard, but even there they might be hours or even days away. And if you get caught in ice,

▶▶ Bob on the summit plateau of Ptlolo on Northumberland Island, North West Greenland.

you can't expect to be rescued by an icebreaker. There have been examples of icebreakers coming to rescue trapped yachts, but that is not something you can demand or expect. You can only wish for it – and be fully prepared to cope with the situation yourself without any outside assistance. And to be towed by an icebreaker can be a frightening experience in itself.

Hospitals and doctors

Be sure to map out where hospitals and medical centres are along your planned route. Gather contact information for them, and it might also be a good idea to have contact with a doctor back home, or even better an experienced expedition doctor who has been out in the wilderness before, so that you can call to get advice if required.

Crew exit points

If you have crew on board who are on a tight schedule – which you should avoid in the first place, if at all possible – be sure to have information on all nearby airports, helicopter services or small plane companies who can reach you if you run out of time. It will of course run the costs through the cabin roof – but that's the crew's choice. No crew should come on board without accepting the fact that he or she might not be able to reach their designated flight or other means of transportation out. The high latitudes are highly unpredictable, unforgiving – and in total command.

Shipyards/haul-out possibilities

Getting a haul out in remote places can often be very expensive, if it is possible at all. All things related to having the boat out of the water should be done before you leave the more civilised parts of the world. But nonetheless – you should have a clear view of where it might be possible to get the boat out on dry land for emergency repairs, or even to leave the boat for the winter (eg Cambridge Bay in the Northwest Passage). Divers can also be a possibility – or bring your own diving equipment to fix a fouled propeller or a rudder that won't function properly.

CREW PREPARATION

The aims and expectations of the crew must be in line to accomplish on-board harmony. Crew might have different expectations on signing up for an expedition to the high latitudes. Once on board, you or anybody else have nowhere to run if relationships don't pan out as expected. That's why it is very important to clarify expectations:

- Why do you want to be part of the crew and cruise?
- How will you contribute?
- What are your strong points and what are your weak points?

It would be helpful to get a firm grip on who knows what and what they are comfortable doing on board. Give everyone responsibilities and try rotating those during long voyages so that everyone can learn new things and feel more confident.

It is also important to go through the whole boat with everyone so that they know where such things as communications, first aid kit, through hull valves, shut-off valves for gas, heating etc are located. Also, prepare them for being locked off from social media and communication services generally, eg Facebook, phone etc. What they see on board is what and whom they will get for the duration of the expedition.

People react differently when they venture to remote areas. The usual negative symptoms are signs of being reclusive, aggressive and seasick, and not necessarily all of the above at the same time. It is usually those who are flown in to the boat and start on a long trip to remote areas such as Antarctica without the possibility to adapt and get familiarised before they leave who are most affected.

Man overboard practice is also something that you should do with new crew. Prepare and explain the on-board routines you use for getting crew back on board if you have a MOB incident. Give clear instructions on what everybody on board should do, and how, and in good weather get one of the crew to get kitted up in a survival suit and jump overboard. The exercise usually gives everybody a very clear understanding of why it is very important to stay on board at all costs.

Novara in scenic Wirik Bay, South Georgia.

4

PREPARING
THE BOAT

THE BOAT ITSELF

There is no such thing as a perfect boat. All boats are the result of a series of compromises. It comes down to the size of your wallet, how many people you are going to take, how long you plan to be away, and – not least – where you are going. But if one were to describe the perfect yacht for a two-month-long high latitudes expedition with two to four people, and money were no object, my suggestions would include the following:

HULL AND DECK

Aluminium or steel? Unpainted aluminium is preferred as it is nearly maintenance free – no polish. Steel, if not treated properly, will eventually rust; but on the other hand, it will stand up to most forces, and it is cheaper. (See later discussions here, and Chapter 5, Sailing in ice.)

'Steel is real', an offshore friend of mine wisely said. They have sailed thousands of nautical miles and even overwintered in their steel boat in Antarctica. With all the debris floating around in the world's oceans as well, it might be wise to choose either aluminium or steel boats when planning to sail in the high latitudes. But the main point is that the hull has to be structurally sound and safe.

All hull through fittings need to be checked and evaluated. If you even think that a valve should be replaced – do it. This reflects sailing in general. If you only think about it, it is not worth much – just do it.

◀◀ Sailing in snowstorms can be a new experience.

▲ Full insulation from the waterline upwards will keep condensation to a minimum and the heat at maximum. Don't forget something for the cabin sole – Bob, wintering in Greenland, said his body was warm, but his feet were cold! Insulation will also keep your boat cool when you are sailing in warm waters.

DECKHOUSE

You can be as tough as you want, but the constant cold and wind will eventually wear you down. If you have an inside steering position, you can sail for longer, in more comfort. The alternative is to build a hard dodger on your existing boat (see Chapter 5). A hard dodger provides more shelter than the usual soft sprayhood, and Plexiglass or hardened glass also gives you a better view.

The hard dodger may also allow you to install solar panels on top. And you can design a canvas cover on the back of the hard dodger to keep the elements out and the warmth inside.

If you install a remote for the autopilot and the chart plotter under the hard dodger, you will be able to sail longer and at the same time be more relaxed. If you are using windvane steering, a short trip out in the open is all it takes to adjust the course.

Tartarooga is one producer of custom-built hard dodgers and biminis, and their site is a good inspiration if you want to take the building matter into your own hands: www.tartarooga.com.

Ocean Navigator also has a good article about how to build a hard dodger in aluminium: www.oceannavigator.com/Web-Exclusives-2013/ Hard-dodger-building-logistics/

HEATING

Full insulation from the waterline upwards keeps condensation to a minimum and the heat at maximum. Don't forget something for the cabin sole – Bob, wintering in Greenland, said his body was warm, but his feet were cold! Insulation also keeps your boat cool when you are sailing in warm waters.

The metal frame on the hatches always leads to condensation. Using thin plastic film to make an airlock will get the water on the framing to freeze and not drip all over the place, or try bubble plastic for those hatches you may need to open from time to time. But then you have to wipe off the condensation that melts.

A Refleks, Dickinson or Taylor's diesel heater with day tank is the preferred heating source. That way you will not need any electricity to keep the temperature up as the heater is gravity fed. The diesel burners also keep the boat relatively dry as they burn up the moist air. Consider central heating with warm-water radiators if you have a larger boat. Whether to keep a diesel heater on when sailing is debatable, as you might experience turbulent air being pressed down the chimney and putting out the fire. The result is a cabin stinking with diesel and exhaust.

RIG

A cutter rigged ketch is the traditional choice, and it gives you more sail configuration options and smaller sails that are easier to handle.

The more modern approach is a cutter rigged sloop as it is easier to handle when short-handed. In harsh climates you often end up sailing short-handed because the rest of the crew needs to rest or are seasick. This is when it is crucial to have an easy setup that you know and can handle on your own.

Standing rigging

A wise person puts cable ties on all shackles to prevent them from loosening. Check every terminal. If you see rust or loose strands, change the standing rigging. If you have rod rigging on your boat, change it to wire. Rod breaks without any warning and you can't use the broken rod for anything. A wire will usually give a sign of wear and tear by either rust or broken strands near the terminal fitting. Make sure you remove things such as old tape to enable a proper inspection of the areas most prone to hazard.

Go aloft to check for cracks in spreaders, terminals and mast all the way to the top. Lubricate all movable parts in the mast while you are up there.

It is good practice to check standing rigging often on passage as well, even if only from the deck. Binoculars can be useful here for the above deck rigging.

Norseman Swageless Rigging Terminals let you do the rigging job yourself. And if you have a rig failure in the high latitudes it might save your trip, or the boat, if you can fix a broken standing rigging. Google DIY Wire Rigging to learn more.

Running rigging

Crossing oceans and sailing for days on end takes its toll on all the equipment. Running rigging is especially exposed during long-distance sailing, and when sailing in the high latitudes it is easy to become somewhat negligent about inspecting all the running rigging due to the cold. It's seldom very comfortable to go on the foredeck in all sorts of weather to see if there are any signs of chafe – but do it anyway. Check all running rigging frequently for chafe. Typical chafing points are where the halyards are locked on the rope jammers. To prevent this, you can sew on a larger diameter rope cover in the exposed area, or use duct tape temporarily. The end of the halyard where the sail is attached is also a risk area. If you have some extra metres on your halyard, it is wise to cut 20–30cm (8–12 inches) off this end every year to prevent it from breaking.

SAIL CONFIGURATIONS

I'm an old regatta sailor who likes to play around with and test different sail options. It keeps me busy, gets the boat going faster and it can make life on board more comfortable.

Dead downwind, I pole out the genoa on a fixed spinnaker pole. That way I can easily reduce the sail area without having to bother about the spinnaker pole. It just stands there until I find it safe to take it down. And I can roll the sail in and out without it furling badly or having to go on the foredeck every time.

Modern boats are usually set up with backswept spreaders. This makes the rig simpler and thereby cheaper. Not a bad thing of course, but not so good if you intend to do some serious sailing — sailing dead downwind we usually want to sail wing-to-wing style, goose-winged, with the genoa poled out to one side and the main

▼ Crossing oceans and sailing for days on end takes its toll on all the equipment. Running rigging is especially exposed during long-distance sailing, and when sailing in the high latitudes it is easy to become somewhat negligent about inspecting all the running rigging due to the cold.

on the other side. With backswept spreaders you won't be able to get your mainsail as far out as you would like. This leaves you with three alternatives: 1) rig twin headsails on two poles, 2) fly a sail like the Parasailor (www.istec.ag) or 3) just bite the bullet and sacrifice 1–2 knots of boat speed.

If you are looking to buy a new boat, or a new rig, intended for offshore and high latitude sailing, I would most definitely recommend a rig with straight spreaders, and personally I would either buy or refit a ketch solution. A ketch rig gives you more sail options to play with – the masts are lower on a sloop, and therefore will not catch the stronger winds higher up. This is of course good when the wind is blowing hard, not so good in the light stuff. Two masts also give you the opportunity to mount radar and/or a wind generator on the mizzen (aft mast), and perhaps to use the boom as a crane to lift on board dinghies, engines, fuel and the like.

An inner forestay where you can have a hanked-on or a roller reefing staysail is much sought after as it gives you more leverage, and brings the centre of effort back on the boat. The hanked-on solution makes it easy to lower and hoist if you leave it hanked on – the size of the sail is usually sufficiently small that it just falls on deck and you can leave it there until a more convenient moment for tidying it up. Bob Shepton did this often when rounding Cape Horn against the wind in the early 90s, before he had roller reefing. A roller reefing inner headsail makes life easier still, as long as you look after it and secure the reefing, or furling, line properly.

SAILS

Dacron yankee, mizzen, main, cutter and storm sails. Gennaker on spinnaker pole. Nowadays, with stronger sail cloth, some prefer a mainsail with four reefs where the fourth reef is the storm sail. Or use a dedicated trysail to save your mainsail. The cutter staysail is either rigged with a roller or on hanks. Hanks is the more secure choice as the roller can unfurl in lots of wind when you have the sail halfway rolled up, and it is easy to set up a smaller headsail on hanks when a big blow is expected or upon you. But again, if you make sure you keep your furling line well secured, to have a rolling inner foresail/storm sail makes life easier still, unrolling and rolling it up from the cockpit, and saves going forward to a bouncing foredeck. But it must be well secured.

Sails in the high latitude are all about durability. I know sailors who have been advised by sailmakers to buy expensive laminate sails for a high latitude expedition. One of them returned with only the storm sail intact. All the other sails had been delaminated and destroyed by the constant beating and sunlight.

Dacron sails still do the trick as they are very durable, and they can be fixed with tape, sticky-back (sailcloth with glue on one side) and needle and thread. Make sure you have a sailmaker's glove, a set of needles and thread on board. Stock up on sail tape and buy some sticky-back from your sailmaker.

Be sure to cover up the sails when not in use as the UV light takes its toll on them and there is more UV in polar regions.

If you have the space and wallet, a sewing machine can save you both time and money; www.sailrite.com sells very good sewing machines that you can have on board, and they can also be operated without electricity.

THE BASICS

Your boat is your home and your lifeline. Make sure it is in the best possible state before you cast off on your adventure. If you have the three basics in good order, you will manage most things: the *rig* will make sure your *hull* keeps moving through the water and the *steering* will keep you in the right direction. Everything else is just nice to have. Think about it. When you sail to places like Ushuaia, Greenland or Svalbard, you very seldom find off-the-shelf production new boats. You will find the oceans' 4x4s built like tanks. They look the business, and won't win any beauty contest. But experienced sailors will always go for strong and practical before four toilets and a built-in espresso machine. Every time. They see the beauty in the functionality. Standard production boats can in general do a trade wind round-the-world trip without too much trouble. It's downwind sailing in warm climates and almost anything will do. But that's not the case in the high latitudes. The conditions are too harsh and you have to be utterly self-reliant. Complex systems are not the way to go here. Keep it simple, and you have to be able to fix it yourself – or manage without it until you reach a place where they have 7-Eleven and McDonald's. That's when you know you are back in civilisation.

But all this is just a dream for most people. The perfect boat is usually the one you have and know, and can bring up to standard. It is at least the boat you are able to afford and know how to sail on a big adventure. Just to make it clear: having made all the above ideal suggestions, there are still a lot of standard production boats that have made and are still making expeditions to the high latitudes, perhaps with slight modifications and additions in some cases.

Stability

The boat has to be stable. The experienced charter skippers working in Antarctica and the Southern Ocean have been, or have friends that have been, pitchpoled or rolled at least once in their career. Then you have to be certain that the boat will eventually end up the right way up.

Having said that, there are a lot of lifting keel boats that sail in the high latitudes. The most famous of them all is *Damien II*, designed by sailing legend Michel Joubert and sailed by Jerome Poncet, for many years the guru of Antarctic sailing. Another variant is the Ovni series. ARC founder and round the world veteran Jimmy Cornell has sailed in both Antarctica and the Arctic with an Ovni 43, though he has just had a new boat designed and built for the next circumnavigation via the high latitudes – the Garcia Exploration 45.

▼ The boat has to be stable. The experienced charter skippers working in Antarctica and the Southern Ocean have been, or have friends that have been, pitchpoled or rolled at least once in their career.

But again, GRP production yachts suitably equipped or modified have sailed in Antarctica and rounded Cape Horn, and one has just completed the Northwest Passage both ways (see Chapter 5, Sailing in ice).

Strength

You might end up getting a serious beating in the high latitudes. It's all mathematics really – the longer you sail, the more experience you will gain. Mostly this is good, but some of it won't be so good. And that's what makes the good stories.

I suggest you make a 'Must have' and a 'Nice to have' list. There are a lot of electronics and electronic gadgets that tend to end up on the 'Must have' list, which then in turn may need revising. It is important to remember that the more things you install, the more complex systems get and the more time you have to spend fixing them when they break down – because something eventually will. Another important aspect is the economic side of it all. You can spend a lifetime installing things you don't need and too much money on it all – money and time you could have spent exploring and gathering memories for life.

Tanks

This is of course all dependent on how remote and how long your expedition will be. If your plans are to sail the Norwegian coast in wintertime, you will have to search a little bit extra to find fresh water. But you will find it on the fishing docks, and everything else is at hand without too much trouble. However, if you are going to the Antarctic Peninsula and from there via South Georgia to Cape Town, we are talking about no diesel for the water maker or ice melting to resupply the water tanks. For such a journey it would be good to have 1,000–2,000 litre diesel, 1,000 litre water and 60–100 litre black water tanks with a crew of four to six, but most boats do not have this ideal. Containers stored on deck can help, with fuel especially, but it is important to have power-saving facilities.

Keel

A shallow draught fixed keel is one option preferred by some when cruising in high latitudes. It is cheaper than a lifting keel, there are no mechanics involved and you can get in to most areas. A lifting keel lets you explore uncharted areas and gets you into even shallower water, which can be useful for skirting round pack ice close inshore. But it might not be necessary for most of the high latitude cruising you have in mind.

Dinghy

For the most remote locations it would be wise to carry two inflatables – the main one preferably in Hypalon, which better withstands UV light and general wear and tear. An outboard that powers the dinghy through high winds is also recommended, as you'll discover when you are trying to get lines ashore fast with a 9.9 hp outboard. An outboard is also a must if you don't want to be stuck on shore because a big onshore blow keeps you from getting back to the boat.

Two dinghies and two outboards might be too much for most boats as they take up quite a lot of space. An inflatable, foldable kayak might be a good second boat, and it will also give you a chance to explore and experience the high latitudes in a very silent and intimate way. Plus, it is good exercise.

It could be argued that every yacht should be built around the dinghy, because the dinghy is the key to all shore-based activities in remote areas. If you lose the dinghy, you are basically stuck on the boat, and might as well sail back home – though some crews have swum ashore for the sake of it! Or let time work with you and build your own dinghy out of driftwood, sails and gaffa tape.

The dinghy is not only for exploring, it is also a vital safety element. You use it to set lines ashore, haul out water and diesel

Never tow the dinghy for long stretches – you could lose it. Nor do you want a curious polar bear or leopard seal to bite through it. Hoist it on board, on deck or in the targa, every night.

to the boat, to check out anchorages before you venture into them with the yacht, and much more. That's why you should take extra good care of your dinghy in the high latitudes. Never tow the dinghy for long stretches – you could lose it. Nor do you want a curious polar bear or leopard seal to bite through it. Hoist it on board, on deck or in the targa (arch on the back of the boat), every night. If you leave the dinghy on the beach, it is wise to put up tripwires connected to flares to scare off polar bears. They usually destroy everything they check out, so beware.

Hypalon dinghies are more durable than ordinary dinghies and accept more beating and sunlight. They are more expensive, but it is worth considering.

Dinghies are fragile, and repeated landings on beaches or over rocks takes their toll. I know you are supposed to carry the boat, but if there are only two of you one seldom does, because it is heavy work. One good solution that will prevent holes in the dinghy and split bottoms is to mount foldable wheels on the transom. Just lower them when you get near the beach and one or two people can easily roll the boat up on the beach. Be sure to roll the boat well over the high tide mark so that waves from calving ice won't reach it.

Best always to tie it to something. And be sure to carry a dinghy repair kit on board.

Steering

You don't need much boating experience to realise that sound and reliable steering is essential for a long-distance cruiser. There have been several incidents in the last few years where the rudder shaft has worked itself loose, chewing through the hull, and in the worst case resulting in the boat sinking.

Check the rudder, the shaft, the quadrant and transfer to the wheel or tiller before setting off. Make sure all your bearings are in good shape, and check the rudder stock for wear and tear. Any signs of wear must be taken very seriously and left to professionals to check. All cables must be checked thoroughly, and make sure you have back-up cables if they should fail. Lay in spare cables or necessary replacements before you leave.

Emergency steering

Emergency steering is also a point to focus on. Be sure you have your emergency tiller available, and that it actually fits. On some boats you have to set up a rope and block system to the winches. Get everything ready and test it all before you leave.

If the rudder should fall off, have a plan for what parts to use to make an emergency rudder. Or make up an emergency rudder before you go.

Autopilots

There is nothing as boring as steering hour after hour when offshore, especially if motoring. It can be fun some of the time – but it loses its appeal after a short while. There are more enjoyable things to do on board. That's why we have autopilots.

Nowadays, autopilots are very reliable. They can be one of the most essential items on board, and if you are sailing short-handed the autopilot is an extra pair of hands. It enables you to rest and sleep, and gives you time to do other chores on board.

When sailing in cold weather and your autopilot drive unit is exposed to the elements, there is a possibility that the cold may affect the pilot. The pilots are often treated with very thick grease from the factory, and in the cold it clogs up and destroys the bearings. One solution to this is to heat the drive unit with spillover warmth from the heater or engine.

In any case, you should have a back-up for both the computer and the linear drive. It is expensive, but an autopilot failure has foiled many expeditions.

Self-steering

But what if the electrical system fails or the autopilot breaks down and you don't have a spare? Then you are left with one person on the wheel at all times.

The answer is the good old windvane. It is reliable, doesn't need electricity and never gets tired.

I have used several different models through the years, and don't really have any preferences as I have managed to get the one I have been using on a particular boat to work. It takes a lot of trimming to balance the boat, but once it is done you can sail for days without any adjustments.

I can recommend the site windpilot.com and the book that the Windpilot manufacturer has written. Of course he wants to sell his products, but he offers valuable information on sailing with windwanes, and he has good products. The ebook is available through his website.

If everything else fails, you can try to balance the boat's sail configuration, and set up the tiller or wheel up with a rope or shock cord on the windward side of the steering. Balance the sails, set a steady course with the tiller or wheel, tie off with clove hitches, and go down below and make a cup of tea. When you find the right balance you can sail for days and weeks with this solution as long as the wind remains fairly constant. There is a more complicated solution using the jib or genoa sheets and shock cord to the tiller on the other side, but try this first! Or maybe a windvane, which demands no electrical consumption, with the possibility to connect a simple autopilot when motoring.

Electronics

Have as few electronic gadgets as possible, as it is important to keep electrical consumption to a minimum. Men explored the world with not even a sextant at their disposal. It would of course be utter madness to go back to the past like that, but when you decide what kind of electronics you need, be sure that you don't just end up with a 'nice to have' list. Electronics require electricity and they can be complex and often very delicate instruments that don't exactly thrive in a harsh salt-water environment.

If you were to go a step over paper charts and compass requirements, a Panasonic Toughbook with built-in GPS and satellite connection to download weather and ice reports can be a solution that will get you through most times. It is also important to have a back-up hard disk with all the electronic charts you need.

Electrics

There are two ways to handle the electrical issues of sailing in remote places: produce electricity and use as little as possible. Both strategies should be followed.

A wind generator on the mizzenmast or aft gantry and solar panels on the gantry or deckhouse will produce green energy. The downside to wind generators is that you often prefer to sail downwind, and that means little apparent wind to drive the generator. And when you anchor, you tend to do so in sheltered places.

Sailboats with their rigging and sails often cast a great deal of shadow, and that is not the best environment for solar panels either. But the technology has come on in leaps and bounds in the last few years, and new and improved solar panels only cut out part of their charging cells when in shadow, not the whole panel as they used to. It is best if the solar panels can be tilted towards the sun to get maximum effect.

A combination of wind and solar is a good option. When it is

sunny with no wind you benefit from the solar, and when the wind is howling from a cloudy sky you get energy from the wind generator.

Another option is a hydrogenerator. The towing solution has been around for years and has helped a lot of sailors – and will in the future too, if the price goes down and durability goes up.

Ensure all lights are LED, if possible, as LED lights use very little electricity.

A travel solar panel with a battery pack that charges the laptop, Iridium phone and external GPS is useful in case of total redundancy should the boat's electricity supply fail.

▲ Have as few electronic gadgets as possible, as it is important to keep electrical consumption to a minimum. Men explored the world with not even a sextant at their disposal. It would of course be utter madness to go back to the past like that, but when you decide what kind of electronics you need, be sure that you don't just end up as a 'nice to have' list.

Light and lights

The good thing about sailing in the Arctic and Antarctic is the constant daylight in the summer months. But when the sun starts to set, it gets dark quickly, and in late summer it draws in earlier each evening. And even if the aurora borealis is worth a winter sailing expedition in itself, the green light doesn't give you enough light to see icebergs or navigate in close quarters. LED technology is the way to go due to its very low consumption of electricity.

Some mount a searchlight on the targa or somewhere else on the back of the boat, but end up with shadows from sails and rigging, and reflections from the same will blind the helmsman. If you have a man on the bow, he will get completely blinded when turning towards the helmsman. I have a 2600 lumen LED light that I fix to the pulpit when needed. The 12V cable is stretched across the deck and under the sprayhood, where I have mounted a switch so I don't have to run below to pull the plug every time I turn it on or off. I also have a powerful hand torch/searchlight in the cockpit to light up areas either side of the boat.

Engine

High latitude isn't the place where you want things to break down – at least, not the essentials like the rig, engine and steering. These are the things that have to function on a boat. You can manage without the engine for a while, but if you don't have any alternative ways to charge your batteries you will soon find out how power-draining all your instruments, such as the heater, fridge, PCs, TVs, radio and so forth, actually are.

Another thing to remember in the high latitudes is that everything is far away. You can't really expect a Raymarine expert to just materialise on the guest pier in Ushuaia if you need him.

You will have to rely on your own resources when things go wrong, and if you have to get spare parts or experts to Ushuaia or anywhere else out there, it takes time and a lot of money. That's why it is important to be fully prepared for all eventualities on the adventure.

Change the oil, oil filter, diesel filters and impeller before the trip. Buy double of everything you have just changed – also oil.

Hatches and ports

Double glazing – thin acrylic sheets over hatches and ports – can be simply held in place by magnetic tape or bungee, or duct tape.

FURTHER EQUIPMENT AND ANCILLARIES

WHAT EQUIPMENT DO YOU REALLY NEED?

This is the fundamental question – how much and what equipment should you bring? You can spend a lifetime equipping your boat for the ultimate expedition that never gets off the dock. It is not only economy and time to spare that influence these choices – most of all it is your own and your crew's competence and feelings of security. Some people are happy to sail with a Maxi 77 without more planning and preparation than 'just woke up one morning and felt like it', while others would prefer trailing the Coast Guard in a 62-footer with all the state-of-the-art equipment money can buy. You must decide, but also think of paring down your list to 'what I really need', which might mean more in some respects and less in others. Polar regions can be an unforgiving place to sail – but it is all worth it in the end.

CHARTS

I probably don't need to say this, but in light of developments in recent years, during which time more and more sailors depend on their electronic charts alone, I would strongly recommend getting paper charts for the area you are venturing into, and also to areas where you might end up, as a back-up.

There are a lot of areas in the high latitudes that are still uncharted – at least on electronic charts. And paper charts are a

▲ If you should end up in ice, it is important to slow down to minimise the effects of possible impact. A long plank or boathook or a dedicated tuk – a pole with a metal blade attached, such as the Inuit use to test ice – is essential for pushing ice aside.

critical asset when and if your electrical system fails, or your on-board electronics black out.

But it's not only that. Paper charts are also valuable when it comes to getting an overview of the big picture – and when it comes to planning the voyage in the comfort of your home beforehand, nothing beats the feeling of rolling out big maps on the kitchen table.

Topo maps or Saga maps in Greenland are also very useful – not only for hiking, but also to find out where the local inhabitants live. They also show you where small fresh water rivers run out into the sea. Here you can fill your tanks, and maybe even catch salmon if you are lucky. Saga maps can also be another useful back-up to your chart plotter or nautical charts, though obviously they do not show depths.

INSURANCE

Not every insurance company will insure your boat and crew for the most remote areas of the world, or they will set the insurance fee so high that it makes no sense. Be sure to obtain quotes from different companies to get a fair price, and a company that understands what you are doing, and actually covers the area you are sailing in.

Topsail Insurance in the UK and Pantaenius in Denmark come highly recommended as they specialise in maritime insurance, and have insured boats recently in polar regions.

▼ Icebergs are easy to spot (except in mist), growlers are not.

Icebergs are irresistible to photograph,
but demand respect.

5

SAILING IN ICE

by Bob Shepton

Sailing in ice is not much different from sailing anywhere else – until we define our terms more accurately, perhaps. Really, I would say that sailing properly with sails up in a breeze is only possible with open ice. I remember doing it down the Gerlache Strait in Antarctica, and fun it was; there were bergs and bergy bits around to be avoided, but in no way were we in close ice or pack ice at that stage. And of course one can sail in the open sea with bergs around, though one year in Greenland we had a narrow escape when a big berg suddenly loomed dead ahead out of the mist. But in pack ice we would be using the term 'sailing in ice' loosely, meaning we would really be motoring on engine in all likelihood, with all sails down. One year in Greenland when my engine was giving trouble, I invented the ditty:

> **'Sailing in Greenland without an engine**
>
> **Is not nice**
>
> **Because of the ice'**

And then remarked, but didn't the old masters do that all the time? Yes, but remember, many never came back. So, though for sailing folks it is a terrible thing to have to admit, sailing in ice requires a good, reliable engine, and a crew member on board 'who is good with engines' is worth two on the shore, whether he or she be contactable or not. And in any case, as I am fond of pointing out, in the Arctic there is often either too much wind or too little, and an engine is almost a necessity for making progress in today's terms.

▶▶ Ice on water. Most boats (even GRPs) can push through thin ice to get in and out of anchorages.

CHEAP DIESEL

I am no engineer, but when it comes to engines it is worth making one or two points. Having a number of fuel filters fitted is important, with a stock of filter elements for renewing from time to time. My friend Rich Haworth formerly of High Latitudes always advised people to fit a set of filters back to back, or rather side by side, with a changeover lever so that if you are having trouble with one you can swap over to the other and deal with the recalcitrant member when more convenient, or while the other one is still allowing the engine

to run. Diesel in Greenland is good, clean, and at the moment the only cheap thing in Greenland! In the settlements in Canada and Alaska it also seemed satisfactory, but transiting the Northwest Passage west to east in 2013, we had to do a lot of motoring, and when we took off the bowl of the water separator unit to change the element towards the end, the bowl was full of water. It was colder in the Arctic in 2013 so this may have been due to condensation rather than compromised fuel, as we had constantly run down and refilled the tank, and condensation can occur in a tank when it is not full and the boat is warmer than the outside temperature (hopefully). Incidentally, if leaving the boat anywhere over the winter, or for a lengthy period of time, it is wise always to leave the tank full, or completely empty. But I am sure you knew that…

WHY GRP?

But what of the boat? Clearly, the preferred material for the boat's hull must be steel or aluminium. So why do I have a GRP boat? Simply because that is the only boat I have, and I cannot afford another one. But to encourage any who have a GRP boat and fear sailing in ice is therefore not for them, it is worth pointing out that I have found GRP to be much stronger than you might expect. I remember arriving at the Meek Channel in Antarctica and wanting to get through to what was then the British Antarctic research base of Faraday in the Argentine Islands; the channel was completely full of brash and small growlers, with not a lead to be seen. We did not want to retrace our steps quite a way back and look for another route round, so we pushed gently on the engine into and through this ice with two crew members pushing ice away when and where they could with jib and genoa poles. OK, so it was only brash and growlers, but if you had been down below and heard the noise of the ice scraping along the hull you might have thought your last hour had come, and I was convinced the ice must be scratching the hull disastrously. When we lifted the boat out thousands of miles later in Darwin, Australia, it was the first thing I looked for. Not a scratch. But then old Westerly yachts were laid up quite heavily.

◀◀ *Dodo's Delight* caught in pack ice off Bylot Island, Baffin. Ice can come in very fast on the tide, but can also go out again very fast!

Watch out

What about a direct impact collision with ice then? One dark night I was moored in a cove in Greenland where I was preparing to winter alone. I had run four lines ashore from bow and stern some time back, but now decided to slip all four to get out of the cove. A north wind had been blowing strongly for three days or more, and ice floes, growlers and bergy bits had been brought round the corner into the cove, despite it being two turnings off from the main fjord. Some trick of the tidal currents. By then I had had enough of fending off and being bumped and scraped, and set forth down the main fjord towards Upernavik. Fortunately, it was not completely dark, as the lights of the airstrip on the hill above Upernavik acted as a sort of moon. The fjord was full of growlers and bergy bits and I weaved and dodged my way down it but eventually, despite having some light, I missed seeing a sizeable lump of ice ahead and hit it full on. True, it was with the point of the bow, one of the strongest parts of the boat. Nevertheless, it made a fearful whack and I was sure it must have stove in the bow to some degree. When I got into Upernavik harbour – for a very disturbed night, still with ice floes floating in, as it turned out – and inspected the damage in the morning, there were one or two small nicks in the gelcoat but nothing significant. I still would not make a habit of doing this by choice, though!

◀▼ Ice watch. When sailing in waters with ice and growlers it is advisable to have an ice-lookout at the bow or in the mast to avoid the biggest chunks.

Elephant seals in Wirik Bay, South Georgia.

There have been one or two other close shaves I could mention, such as when I took a shortcut to the Vaigat north of Disko Island with three glaciers calving to the east, which turned out not to be such a good idea. But when all is said and done, given the choice and sufficient resources, going into ice I would choose steel or aluminium. There is one other possibility: when a friend of mine, John Gore-Grimes, who has done a lot of sailing in the Arctic over the years, was having his new Najad constructed in Sweden, he had

▼ It is best to go to windward of icebergs because brash can collect to leeward.

A satphone then is 'almost essential'. It is also useful in case of emergencies. Personally, I have found it is a boon here to purchase a permanent antenna and rig it outside with a cable coming back to the chart table. AST systems supplied mine. It works better and it saves trying to stick the mobile antenna on to a winch or some such every time you wish to use it, or having to go outside to use it. I have also found that whereas using a satphone for voice eats up your minutes' allowance, to use it with a modern email system uses very little owing to its ability to compress and send, and to receive quickly. Again I use the satphone for weather, but this requires someone like the ever helpful Peter Semiotuk, formerly of Cambridge Bay, to keep emailing you weather forecasts. Or you could get your guru to copy GRIB files, or synoptic charts of Greenland's ice or weather, for instance, and send them on the same system as for your ice reports.

And radar can be useful. A friend of mine who has sailed a lot in the Arctic used to say 'men don't need radar'. His boat now has it!

▲ Weaving easily through brash and growlers.

Certainly on our first visit to Greenland, we came down from Iceland and passed close round Cape Farewell, to get up to Qaqortoq (or Julianehab, as it used to be called), and found ourselves in a lot of ice in thick mist. We spent the day steering the boat practically on radar alone, one of us sitting down below and shouting directions up to the helmsman – 'steer to port now, back to starboard now, OK straight ahead for a while, oh, port again' and so on. It was our first experience of ice and our first use of radar and it saved the day for us. Again, skippering someone else's boat one year and coming out of St. John's, Newfoundland, to cross the Atlantic, it was a great comfort to have the radar in the fog that is almost traditional in those parts, and to spot what must have been big icebergs to be avoided out at sea. Or Tash, waking me early one morning off Cape York in Melville Bay, Greenland, where icebergs from the local glaciers meet and the radar looked as if it had caught a dose of measles. Or approaching Northumberland Island in the far north with our newly acquired chart plotter plus radar, and picking up the coastline and anchorage without being able to see anything in the mist until we got right there. Yes, radar can be useful, especially in fog and mist or at night, but you do need calm conditions so that there is little or no sea speckle to confuse the situation. In clear visibility and daylight, eyeballing is better, of course.

GET THE TUK

What else might you need? A tuk, or preferably two, is another essential. A tuk is a metal blade attached to a pole; the Inuit use shorter ones to test ice to see whether it is safe to walk on, and for making holes to catch seals by then shooting a net under the ice attached to a tuk, with its wooden pole bringing it up again in a hole at the far end (very clever), and sailors use longer ones to push ice away. At first it may seem that nothing is moving but as you persist then it will move away – and it is not just your boat moving backwards either, though that is probably happening too. Large lumps of ice can be moved with a bit of effort in this way.

We had a minor complication with this one year in the Tasmanian Islands, off the Boothia Peninsula in north-east Canada and part of the Northwest Passage: an ice floe kept on coming back after we had pushed it away with our tuk. It was not only the awkward tidal currents in that particular cove, it was also caught on our tripping line. In the end, crew member Rich jumped on to the ice floe, we let out more line, he jumped back, we motored close round the floe and eventually managed to hook and flick the tripping line off the floe, which then sailed sedately away.

Why am I telling you this? As a general rule, don't use a tripping line in ice; I had thought we were going to be anchoring in another place with kelp and rocks but that did not work out… Still, that's one better perhaps than when another time we were caught in pack ice off Bylot Island, north of Baffin, moving in very fast. Without further ado, Polly and Tash stripped to their sponsored thermal

▲ Big ice. A boat gets dwarfed among icebergs in Greenland. In daylight and good visibility, it is easy to navigate among icebergs, but watch out for underwater shelves.

Part of an ice shelf off the west coast of Greenland. A different hazard!

underwear and jumped on to a big ice floe for a photo shoot. Probably the best photo shoot that firm has ever had! If you are a big boat with a powerful dinghy and outboard, you can gently ram the bergy bit and push it away with the dinghy and your powerful engine, with or without a tuk.

Be aware too of the danger of getting your anchor stuck under ice floes, or pack ice moving in. One year in the far north of Greenland I came to the conclusion that it was better to abandon anchoring and motor a little way out to sea and just drift in clear patches until it became necessary to turn the motor on again to get to another clear patch, and so on. It saved the rather stressful situation we had just endured of trying to fish our anchor up from under the ice floe that had covered it.

I am assuming you have an EPIRB, preferably with GPS incorporated, and a liferaft on board. And a well-stocked panic bag, should you have to abandon ship. But these are not exclusive to polar regions. However if you do abandon ship in polar regions and step onto an ice floe, please be sure to take the liferaft and gear with you for shelter and safety, as a crew recently did not and were lucky to survive. They lost the boat.

SPARE PROP

On the Northwest Passage transits, I have been carrying a spare prop in case the existing one got damaged by ice – it was quite a drama drying the boat out against a wall in Scotland to get the old one off to measure the required angle and length at the shaft end for the new one. I even carried a chainsaw, which is also still on board, in case we were caught in impenetrable ice. So far I have not had to use either of them, I am glad to say. In 2013 I bought and fitted an electronic autohelm, or rather Rich, our Mr Fixit, fitted it for me. Because there is often either too much wind or too little and you do a lot of motoring in the Arctic and Antarctic, this was to give some relief from hand steering for the crew, whether motoring or sailing. In 2012 we had hand steered across the Atlantic, up the long west coast of Greenland and through the Northwest Passage, so it is possible – but then these climbers are tough! We did have some trouble calibrating this new self-steering, but it certainly proved its worth when we eventually got it working, especially and almost exclusively when motoring. And a word about windvane steering, which you may well use on the ocean and sea approaches but not, I would think, in icy waters themselves. Be careful that you have one where the servo-pendulum rudder can be cocked up or, better still, removed altogether, so that it is clear of the water and not bashed by lumps of ice around you. Beware also, because with some systems the pole or upright to which the servo-pendulum rudder is bolted can itself be on or below the waterline even when the rudder has been removed, and this will then suffer the same fate. Might you have to remove the whole system altogether before you get into ice? It is possible, I gather, but perish the thought; however, it's your decision.

RUDDERS

Talking of rudders, it is wise to have some form of spare or emergency rudder should your boat's main one get bashed, broken or bent.

Again, we have not had to use this so far, for which I am thankful as I am not entirely confident as to how well my home-made wooden emergency rudder system would work.

GETTING CLOSE

So you are in the Arctic or Antarctic and there is ice around. When you first see it on the horizon it appears as a long, white, unbroken, impassable line of ice. The cardinal rule here is: you will not be able to tell what it is really like until you get right up to it. Only then will you be able to see whether there are any leads, and to assess what concentration it is and whether you are likely to be able to get through. We probably went too far south in 2013 when we encountered a long tongue of pack ice off the Bathurst peninsula by Amundsen Gulf coming down from the north, before we turned into it to choose a narrow channel through. We had not initially gone right up close to look. Then, passing through Snowgoose Channel between Bathurst and the Baillie Islands, there was ice on the other side too, which from a distance again looked impassable. Only when we got close did we see it was really only 2/10ths as forecast, and we spent an enjoyable afternoon weaving and dodging our way through to get down to the remote, but safe, enclosed bay of Summer Harbour.

It is ironic that the main aim of an ice pilot is actually to avoid ice, or at least to avoid becoming embroiled in ice that is going to threaten the boat. But if you are in ice it can be useful to have mast steps so that a crew member can climb up the mast and spot leads if it has got that concentrated. A friend of mine, who has a superyacht on which I have worked, tells the story of how when passing through the Prince of Wales Channel in the Northwest Passage in 2012, she sent Hank up the mast to spot the best way through. Hank pointed one way, she, as the lady owner, chose another and steered the boat the opposite way, with Hank still waving frantically from the mast! But that's another thing about ice – everybody has their own, usually different idea of which way you should go. I remember on the same

boat in the Strait of Belle Isle between Newfoundland and Labrador a few years back, it was a dark night and there were big icebergs and smaller bergy bits around. There were five of us up there in the cockpit and I am sure we all had our own ideas of which way we should go. I was steering, and thought we should go to port round the next bit. The skipper shouted across to go to starboard. I went to starboard – it is important in ice to have one person clearly in charge at the time, whether it's the helmsman or skipper, and whose directions are therefore followed without question.

But you are in ice, what should you do? There is not much advice I can give here. Obviously you search for leads of open water to try and get through. You send someone up the mast. You use your tuk, you push gently with your boat. You carry a chainsaw in case of being badly beset. And patience is a virtue … get out on to the pack ice if you are stuck and take pictures of your boat in the ice, and wait. One big lesson in polar regions is: learn to wait. Ice can change, and very quickly sometimes – for better or worse mind you!

But now, with the advent of drones, a whole new revolution is available to us. Fancy being able to launch a small flying object up above the boat that sends pictures back to the boat of the ice ahead, so that we can spot any possible leads through. Huh, it wasn't like that in my day! Mind you, it is important to have worked out how you are going to get the drone back again afterwards!

Have fun: it's challenging, it's enjoyable, and sailing in ice beats the Mediterranean or Caribbean any day. For a start, you may well be the only boat there … which is what it's all about.

Dodo's Delight weaving comfortably through icebergs, West Greenland.

standing watches and helping out on a passage in stage 1. Others will just be useless and lie in their bunk. It's when they reach stages 2 and 3 that you will feel the overall effect. Not only are you one crew fewer to stand watches, cook meals, navigate and do chores, you might also have to look after them actively. Each sick crew member can therefore set you back at best one and a half or even two additional crew. But most crew can look after themselves in these circumstances – give them a bucket and get them into their bunk.

It is also worth pointing out that crew often feel better if they do get up and stand their watches, as it gives them something else to do and think about.

But it is important to get everyone's take on how they usually react to potential seasickness, and to take precautions accordingly. Have an assortment of anti-seasickness pills and remedies on board. On long offshore passages such as the Drake Passage or Denmark Strait, severe seasickness can be a real danger to health and safety as the seasick get dehydrated. Remind them to keep drinking – water or juices.

At night

When at anchor, be sure to put the boarding ladder down. If one of the crew should fall into the water, that little precaution could mean the difference between life and death.

Always think in terms of keeping an anchor watch, but if you are feeling good about the anchorage, weather forecast and anchoring arrangements, you might want to consider not having a physical anchor watch. Sometimes a rested crew is better than sticking to routine.

When using an instrumental anchor watch, it is often better to use the depth alarm over the anchor alarm. As it is not reliant on GPS it can be more accurate and instant, and the noise is louder. But remember to take the tidal effect into account before adjusting the depth alarm. And remember to switch it off in the morning!

As we have seen elsewhere, it is also useful to put the chart plotter on high (or close) resolution. Then the track lines on the chart will

▲ Track lines of the boat at anchor in Tay Bay, Baffin. When wind increased, we let out more chain, hence the second group of track lines.

▶▶ *Dodo's Delight* – an ordinary production GRP Westerly 33, with inner forestay and solid cuddy added, has sailed thousands of miles in the Arctic and Antarctic. It is possible!

pile up into a black smudge as the boat swings to her anchor, and it will be easy to see if and when the track takes off backwards should the anchor happen to drag. If keeping a physical anchor watch, this also saves the watcher having to go up to look around so frequently. We had a prime example on Steve Brown's *Novara* in South Georgia when, in a 75-knot gust, the boat suddenly took off backwards on the chart plotter. A hasty re-anchoring ensued.

First aid

In the high latitudes, search and rescue is at the best of times days away. More often than not you have to rely on your own equipment and knowledge. In terms of first aid, most boats carry the full medical kit described in the *Ship Captain's Medical Guide*, with perhaps the exclusion of oxygen and IV fluids if nobody is trained to administer them. Also carry a couple of good books on wilderness first aid and consider doing a course such as Wilderness First Responder or similar. At least one of your crew or yourself should have completed a basic first aid course, and if it was a few years ago you should take a refresher course.

Consult your regular doctor before an expedition for advice on what medicines you should take with you.

See also the MIN 600 Ships captains medical guide (https://www.gov.uk/government/publications/min-600-ships-captains-medical-guide-23rd-edition).

You can also subscribe to an emergency medicine service (such as www.thefirstcall.com/sea/). Then you will always have an experienced doctor within Iridium phone reach to assist you.

Glaciers

Glaciers fascinate most people but they might be as dangerous and unpredictable as polar bears. Keep the recommended distance of 200 metres from the front of a calving glacier. It is very important to keep a safe distance, as a group of tourists and crew learned the hard way in 2007, when ice falling from Hornbreen in Hornsundet slammed on to the deck of a Russian cruise ship and injured 18 passengers and crew.

It is impossible to predict when calving may occur, the size of the ice block that will fall off, or how it will enter the water. Big blocks of ice falling off the ice front can create a hailstorm of smaller ice bits, which can harm crew and boats close by, while the surge that follows a calving can be dangerous for both small yachts and especially dinghies out exploring. A distance of 200 metres is considered safe in order to avoid both direct hits and the largest waves.

This is what the Norwegian Polar Institute recommends:
- At the level of individual events, calving is a random process. It is impossible to predict precisely when calving may occur, how large a block will be created, or how it will enter the water. 200 metres is a safe minimum distance, with a good margin for safety, for avoiding both direct hits and the largest waves.

Furthermore:
- Using calving cliff height as a means of estimating the minimum safe distance (MSD) is really inadequate since the hinge point

▼ Beware that bits can fall off icebergs at any time.

can lie beneath the waterline. In addition, submarine calving events can bring large ice blocks much farther out than the calving cliff height.

- Waves that are created closest to the block, in the so-called splash zone, are very large, unpredictable and dangerous, particularly for small boats. The MSD for avoiding direct hits from ice blocks needs to be larger to ensure that vessels are outside of the splash zone.
- Outside of the splash zone, waves become more consistent, and can be ridden out. However, as waves become grounded, either in shallow water or on shore, tsunami waves can also be created.
- Small boats should not land on shores near the edge of calving cliff faces.
- The 200 metre distance should be increased in narrow fjords, in shallow fjords, or in locations with ice cliffs higher than 40–50 metres.

When hiking in Svalbard, you might end up wanting to cross or walk on a glacier. Glaciers have crevasses and all walking on glaciers should be done with sufficient safety equipment such as harnesses, ropes and ice axes. You must have a back-up plan for how to hoist a man out of a crevasse if the worst should happen. If uncertain, practise beforehand, or avoid walking on glaciers.

OPERATION PROCEDURES: DINGHY

The dinghy is your most important piece of kit for exploring. If you should lose it, and don't have a second one, it could mean the end of your expedition. It is also one of the most exposed items with regards to accidents such as attack by polar bears, walruses or leopard seals. Falling ice and strong winds are also potential dangers.

- Always let the skipper know when the dinghy is being used, who is on board and where you are planning to go. Bring a VHF and make sure the VHF on the yacht is tuned in to the same channel. It's worth testing them together on the boat before setting off.

▲ Dinghy rides. A good dinghy is essential for exploring, safety, towing icebergs and more. It is even possible to push an ice floe away with a dinghy and outboard engine.

- Bring the emergency barrel (see page 88).
- Make sure the engine is running before you cast off – a simple mistake that is sometimes made!
- Have a contingency plan if the engine fails: drop the anchor, OR row to the nearest shore downwind. Always carry paddles even when using the engine.
- Carry the dinghy well out of the tidewater range.
- Secure it well.
- It's a good idea to clean your boots, to avoid dirt on board, before you step back into the dinghy.

If you are in polar bear country, these rules must also be followed:
- Bring at least one gun.
- Protect it from saltwater spray in the dinghy.

- Keep a sharp lookout on the beach at which you are planning to land. Do not step ashore if you suspect polar bears to be nearby, or if there are obvious hiding places for the bear close by. Polar bears hunt ALL living things.
- Don't load the gun before you are on shore, or 'make safe' if loaded.

On shore

Exploration on shore is one of the reasons we venture into the high latitudes. Security in remote areas is vital, and you would be wise to have a plan and the necessary equipment at hand for most situations. That said, you can't carry a replacement boat on your back every time you go ashore. The following list is substantial and will not suit all. Take this as advice and make your own selection, depending on the circumstances.

Basic rules for travel on shore in bear-infested areas

- Make sure you stay together as a group.
- If you split up, each group must have at least one weapon OR it is recommended that any groups that don't have weapons should at least have a pen flare gun or the like.
- Always keep a vigilant lookout for polar bears and their potential hiding places.
- At least one of you should wear or carry a waterproof survival suit in case you have to swim to the boat. It takes only a few minutes in polar water before you become hypothermic.

Dinghy safe barrel

- Extra VHF with fully charged or extra batteries
- Flares
- Matches
- Food and water
- Multitool
- Dinghy and outboard repair kit
- Vacuum-packed drysuit in case you need to swim back to the boat

▲ Polar bears can pop up unexpectedly!

■ Onshore barrel

This is the extreme variant of 'what if' thinking, but it might save your life if you are in a very remote and cold place. I have friends who have returned to the bay where they anchored their boat before they went onshore for a hike, only to find the bay empty. The offshore wind had blown their yacht to sea. The heavy fog didn't help the search, but luckily they found it just as they were about to give up.

Or what if there is a fire on board and you have to evacuate the boat and watch it burn and sink? Or even the less extreme scenario where the weather turns so bad that the on-board skipper has to leave the anchorage while you are on shore? That's when it pays to be prepared with a set of life-saving spares on board, ready for the shore. The barrel is chosen to keep polar bears out of it. If in Antarctica or polar-bear-free country, other storage alternatives can be used.

Equipment to be stored in the barrel

- Tent
- Sleeping bags
- Sleeping mats
- Cooking equipment and fuel
- Food and water
- Toilet paper
- Matches
- First aid kit
- Solar charging panel with chargeable battery that fits VHF and Iridium

Backpack for shore expeditions

- VHF
- Iridium phone
- Map
- Compass
- GPS
- Shelter of some sort
- Matches

- First aid kit
- Warm clothes
- TPA (Thermal Protective Aids) or one-piece immersion suits

NB: And we always carry at least one shotgun/rifle and the ones without have flares. You don't need a gun in Antarctica as there are no polar bears.

▲ The silent way. If you have room for kayaks onboard you will get both exercise and a whole new way of exploring the areas up close.

On the boat
Grab bags for emergencies
Items from around the boat, which of course may be in general use but should be considered for the grab bag or such a list, are:
- Handheld VHF (fully charged/spare batteries where appropriate)
- Handheld GPS (fully charged/spare batteries where appropriate)
- EPIRB/PLB

▶ A walrus basking alone in the sun on an ice floe.

▼ Tracker. The Spot tracker is an affordable satellite safety device, delivering reliable location-based tracking, messaging and S.O.S. technology.

- Seasickness tablets
- Torch
- Extra flares
- TPA (Thermal Protective Aids) or one-piece immersion suits

Warm clothing, glasses and essential medication might make the time you spend in the liferaft easier and beyond this there are also items that, while not essential, will make your life a lot easier once back on dry land. These include:
- Passport
- House/car keys
- Wallet/credit cards
- Mobile phone
- Ship's documents

Think of taking those one-gallon water containers with you.

OPERATING PROCEDURES IN POLAR-BEAR TERRITORY

Greenland, North Canada, North Russia and Svalbard are polar bear territory, and since the white bear has no natural enemies he regards these regions as his own. In Longyearbyen on Svalbard, all people venturing outside the inner city limits have to carry a weapon – and know how to use it. Canada also virtually insists on you carrying a rifle in arctic regions and charges comparatively little for a permit – obtainable when you check in. Certain areas such as parts of the Northwest Passage and the Northeast Passage also have a high density of polar bears.

Advice from the Norwegian Polar Institute states the following:

'The bear's behaviour often reveals whether it is curious or aggressive. A curious bear will usually approach slowly. It will pause, stretch its neck and sniff. The head and neck weave from side to side, and bob up and down.

▲▼ Warning. You have to expect Polar Bears everywhere on Svalbard. Be prepared.

Polar bears on pack ice
75-miles off Clyde River,
Baffin Island.

An aggressive bear is more assured in its movements. It may attack without warning, but sometimes gives various attack signals. It can, for example, snort through its nose, or snap its teeth with a smacking sound. In that event one should be particularly on guard. The attack often comes very quickly. The bear takes a course directly towards its prey at a quick trot, or in big bounds.

Always carry a weapon with you in areas where polar bears might be encountered. Stay calm if a bear approaches. Keep your weapon ready. If you think the situation is becoming dangerous, toss away your mittens, hat, scarf, or something similar. The bear might stop and sniff at the garments, giving you a chance to get to safety. If you have time, fire some warning shots at the ground in front of the bear.'

In order to gain the maximum experience in the Arctic – including, of course, good polar bear sightings – it is necessary to follow some basic safety procedures. Inevitably each and every bear encounter will require specific action, but the following is intended as an outline.

Read more in my book *Sail to Svalbard* (Jon Amtrup, 2012) and at www.cruise-handbook.npolar.no/en/_

Weapons

On Svalbard you are required to carry a weapon at all times when on shore. Weapons can be rented in Longyearbyen, at Sportscenteret and Ingeniør G. Paulsen.

▶ Essentials shore gear. Ice axe, charts and ammunition.

In Greenland it is not usual to carry a gun for polar bear protection, but it may be advisable in remote areas in east Greenland and in the far north. Guns and ammunition can be bought in the main store in every settlement or second-hand from KIK-IND, a shop in Sisimiut. Choose a weapon within a minimum calibre of 30-06. Anything smaller will not stop the bear – just make him angry. Use full metal jacket bullets for the rifle and slugs if you have a shotgun.

Make sure you know how to operate the gun, and practise target shooting. When or if a bear suddenly appears it is too late to try to find out where the safety catch is. Polar bears are a threatened species so try at all costs to avoid killing one. Shoot warning shots; make lots of noise to try to scare the bear off before it gets too close to create a dangerous situation, fire flares. But if push comes to shove and you have to shoot to kill, it is highly advisable that you shoot quickly. They can move very fast.

If you are unfortunate enough to have to kill a polar bear, you must report it to the authorities at the earliest opportunity.

▲ Make sure you know how to operate the gun and practise target shooting.

Dodo's Delight playing Moses with the icebergs.

circumnavigation of Svalbard and it did provide tracking all the way.

inReach goes one step further as it is a two-way satellite communication tool, and it uses Iridium, so it guarantees coverage on both poles and in between. You can also subscribe to weather information through the system. It does the same as SPOT, but if you download an app to your phone you can send and receive email and SMS through the satellite system. The Garmin inReach SE is an all-in-one device that doesn't need the app for texting.

This is a very affordable way to stay in contact, keeping a high focus on security at the same time.

But all this presupposes your budget runs to the type of satphone that has a tracking device. Other satellite phones can still use email through a laptop with a suitable marine server.

◀◀ A pleasant day in Greenland after climbing.

SSB

The growth of satellite communication has reduced the use of SSB, but it is still a very useful way of communicating. You can listen in on nets and other sailors in your area discussing weather, ice and cruising conditions, download weather reports and listen to

▼ The 'sword of Damocles' of ice that nearly prevented us from setting out of Prince Regent Inlet on the Northwest Passage.

radio when off the beaten track; it also lets you send and receive mail, if you have a suitable modem. And it's all for free, when you have paid for the machine and done the course to obtain your licence. But they are quite expensive.

Mail via SailMail or Winlink works well in most areas of the world and has global coverage, necessary for the Northwest Passage, and works well on the Antarctic Peninsula. The Airmail software also has a very good interface for requesting GRIBs and a built-in viewer. UUPlus is another system that works well.

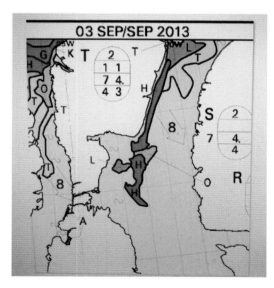

Mist below glaciers, Devon Island.

8 WEATHER

■ WEATHER ROUTING

Shore-based weather routing has developed quickly in recent years, and there are a lot of companies and weather gurus, more or less experienced, who offer these services. But the decision whether or not to use them, or to take their advice if you do, is always yours, and be sure to talk to the weather router before you hire them. It is important that they gain knowledge about how prepared the boat and crew are, and that they know how much weather you are prepared to tackle. Inform the weather router of how the boat handles under different circumstances, what kind of sails you have and how fast your boat is sailing in different wind conditions, all important considerations.

It is also good to check references to make sure that they are the real stuff.

I have used a few different weather routers on various offshore passages in my time, and I have never done exactly as they have advised. Again, it is important to remember that in the end it is you,

▶ Hove-to in an Atlantic gale.

as skipper, who are responsible for all decisions and you have the best feel for the boat and the weather you are in. I have used my knowledge of the boat and crew, downloaded other GRIB files and weather information, watched the barometer and sailed accordingly. Having said that, I have never diverged hugely from the advice weather routers have given. They have mostly been spot on. But if you are cruising in polar regions you may prefer to make your own decisions as you have more challenging conditions with wind, waves, current and possible ice.

Weather4expeditions
www.weather4expeditions.com
Commanders' Weather
www.commandersweather.com
Weather Routing Inc.
www.wriwx.com
WeatherGuy
www.weatherguy.com
Navimeteo
https://www.navimeteo.com/marine-weather/

DO-IT-YOURSELF WEATHER ROUTING

I always gather as much information about the weather as I possibly can before I cast off. This includes following the weather system at least one week before departure, and then downloading the latest GRIB files and local weather reports before we slip out of GSM range. On long offshore passages of more than two to three days, I download GRIB files via satellite or get friends ashore to send me text messages with weather over Iridium or the inReach two-way satellite communication device I always have on board. Or friends can send via whatever email system you have on board.

If you want to interpret weather charts and weather in real time, I highly recommend Steve and Linda Dashew's *Mariner's Weather Handbook*. A free download is available on www.setsail.com

▲ Sturdy. Aluminium is a preferred material among many high-latitude sailors.

But weather forecasting in the high latitudes is still unreliable, and no single source of forecast gets it right all the time. The weather systems frequently move either more slowly or more quickly than expected. Sometimes the sequence is right, the timing is not. Lows can quickly develop out of what for a layman seems like nowhere, and high-pressure systems can stall and block an incoming low.

The best approach is to keep track of the barometer every hour; matching it up to the various forecasts then gives you a more precise view of how quickly systems are moving and what is likely to happen next. The more you pay attention to the forecasts and how they match up with real weather and the barometer, the more knowledgeable and confident you will become. And remember to study the sky…

WHAT ARE GRIB FILES?

GRIB is the format the meteorological institutes of the world use to transport and promulgate weather data, and is the foundation of most of the forecasts we see in our daily life. They can be obtained free and many sailors use them as a low-cost way of getting a lot of weather information. Once downloaded, you will see GRIB files in the form of weather arrows indicating heading and strength of the wind overlaid on a chart. The files show how the wind develops over the coming hours or days. The higher the resolution, the more accurate are the predictions.

The GRIB files also give information on rain, barometric pressure, cloud cover, air temperature at sea level and wave height.

▼ Packed in. Snow, wind and ice are not a good combination when you have to stand still most of the time.

GMN Marine Weather Services

Free software that works very well on satellite uplink as the file sizes are small.

http://www.globalmarinenet.com/free-grib-file-downloads/

PredictWind

www.predictwind.com

Theyr.com

www.theyr.com

Windy

www.windy.com

zyGrib

Open source and very comprehensive GRIB viewer.

www.zygrib.org

NOAA's Weather Fax Service

HF FAX weather charts good in Canada, Pacific side of Antarctic Peninsula, and for NZ and Australian Antarctica.

https://www.weather.gov/marine/radiofax_charts

Saildocs

Essential weather resource can provide GRIBS from several different models.

www.saildocs.com

Chile Navy Weather Service

Ice charts for Antarctic Peninsula and synoptic forecasts etc.

http://web.directemar.cl/met/jturno/indice/english.htm

Mobile apps

iOS

Mac apps for GRIB format:

- iGrib
- PocketGrib
- WeatherTrack
- Weather4D

Android

Android apps for GRIB format:

- mobileGRIB
- PocketGrib
- SailGrib
- Weather4D

9 ANCHORING AND MOORING

When anchoring in high latitudes you often have a combination of strong winds, tidal currents, exposed anchorages, and rocky, kelp-covered bottoms to contend with. That is something completely different from what most people are used to, and the challenge should not be taken lightly. Ground tackle that has worked well for years in temperate and tropical waters may prove inadequate in the high latitudes.

The best advice is to keep it simple, get at least one modern anchor, such as Spade or Rocna, pick one size bigger than the manufacturer recommends, and stick to the solutions that you know work for you.

Have at least three anchors when sailing in the high latitudes. Not only for the risk of losing one – if you have only one and lose it, your expedition is over – but also so you have the possibility of putting out extra anchors in a big blow. Use 60–100 metres of anchor warp and a short length of chain attached to the main anchor (less overall length if chain is used all the way), and 50–100 metres of warp and a short length of chain for the kedge anchor.

▲ Tied in. Use a snubber line to protect your windlass.

Let out at least 5:1 of the depth you are anchoring in, maybe less for chain all the way, and back up until the boat doesn't move. Now you have to pay attention to possible wind shifts, drifting ice that can take out your anchor chain or boat, and gusting winds. Be sure to have one person on board at all times to make sure the boat is OK. There are a lot of examples of the whole crew going ashore only to come back to the beach to find the boat either gone or well up on the beach, on its side.

In the high latitudes you end up anchoring in places where you wouldn't ordinarily even consider spending the night given normal conditions. But there is very little up here that is normal when it comes to cruising. That's why we come here.

Anchoring is a question of minimising risk as much as you can, to get as much adventure as you can at the same time. It's all a question of imagining worst-case scenarios and thinking 'what if…'. You have to evaluate if the anchor is reasonably attached to the bottom, and if the wind is going to change.

It is also advisable to have one or more lines that are 100 metres long, or two or three that you can tie together, so that you can also tie the boat to land in tight spaces.

It is advisable always to use either an anchor alarm or a depth alarm when at anchor. Set the alarm extra loud. If the weather is unsettled you should also consider setting anchor watches with the crew in rotation, or use a wake-up alarm every hour to check the boat and surroundings.

As mentioned before, it is also useful to set the chart plotter to a high (close) resolution, and the track lines will pile up together on the plotter as the boat swings on her anchor. It will then be easy to see the track line take off backwards if the anchor drags.

Holding in high latitudes can be bad as there is no vegetation on the bottom and therefore very little mud; there is clay in some places, but often just rock. Or there is kelp, which is a vegetation you do not want!

▲ *Dodo's Delight* anchored in thin ice in Stella Creek, Antarctica. 'We virtually threw the anchor over the bow. We knew we were not going anywhere that night'.

If there is a serious amount of pack ice or ice floes around, consider another alternative to anchoring, as described in Chapter 5, Sailing in ice.

TYPES OF ANCHOR

Fisherman's

This design has been used by sailors for hundreds of years and was perfected in England in the 18th century. Nothing beats weight to cut through kelp and find a purchase on an uneven bottom. Big heavy fisherman's anchors are still popular among some high latitude sailors as they cut through kelp and hook into rock very well. The downside is that they are very difficult to stow on board when not in use. Perhaps consider this as a secondary anchor to a modern anchor like Spade or Rocna when sailing in areas like Greenland and Svalbard, where the kelp and rocks sometimes make it challenging to anchor.

▶It is important to carry at least three anchors (preferably four) in polar regions. Here a CQR is still a back-up to a Rocna and Delta.

Spade

This is an anchor from the late 1990s, which like the CQR and Delta has only one tip, but the concavity is inverted to be spoon-like. As the concave profile moves through the bottom, it is designed to compact the sea-floor material within its form, rather than sliding through it like a plough. Nearly 50 per cent of the anchor's total weight is applied on to the tip when the rode pulls on the shank. The goal of the design is to penetrate the sea floor, even into hard sand and through weeds. Spade recommends a slightly heavier anchor per boat length than Delta, but offers an aluminium version at less than half the weight of its steel offering.

CQR

The plough is a seasoned design from the early 1930s, with characteristics of a hooking anchor and plough-shaped flukes for holding in soft sand and mud. The hinged shank allows a wide degree of effectiveness, but it may not reset well if it does break free. This anchor relies on weight to penetrate the bottom: the heavier it is, the more firmly it will set. The more scope the better.

Delta

This design is a hybrid combining the best of the CQR design and the Bruce. A one-piece steel casting, it is a hooking anchor in many ways similar to the Bruce. It has a weighted point for penetrating mud, hard sand bottoms and kelp, which gives it more versatility. Like the CQR, it has flukes for holding in sand and mud, but the Delta's flukes are more obliquely angled and therefore present a broader, flatter surface than does the CQR, providing greater potential holding for the same size and weight. It was suggested as the best anchor in the more moderate price ranges tested, before the better but more expensive anchors (*Yachting Monthly*, July 2013).

Bruce

Originally designed in the early 1970s, this is a one-piece cast steel anchor that is both strong and versatile. Huge versions are used to secure giant drilling platforms in the North Sea. With its three-pronged hooking design, this anchor grabs coral and ledge very well, and its wide shape helps it to bury itself in the sand or mud. Its design makes it easy to set and it holds at its maximum loading on quite short scope, 4:1 or even 3:1. Because it sets easily and quickly, it also resets easily when the wind or current changes.

Rocna

This is one of the new generation anchors, offering the best features of the Delta and the Spade. The design offers concavity for holding power and superior penetration ability from its contoured bottom. A roll bar prevents the anchor from dragging on its side or upside down. It resets quickly in most situations. But it is expensive.

Fortress

This is a well-proven lightweight anchor made of aluminium. It is notable for its high weight to holding ratios. It has adjustable flukes, enabling you to set it either for sand and shell bottoms or for soft mud bottoms. In the latter conditions, ooze and swamp mud, the Fortress may have no equal. This anchor disassembles and folds for storage.

These anchors vary enormously in cost. In the end it is probably a combination, or compromise, between cost and holding power that will dictate what anchors you carry.

MOORING LINES

Four mooring lines of 100–120 metres are a necessity if you are planning to spend a season in the Chilean channels, Antarctica or Greenland. In most situations, floating lines like polypropylene or Spectra are preferable to nylon. These lines don't absorb water, so they remain lightweight, easy to handle from the dinghy and relatively free of kelp.

But when you have to anchor in ice, it is preferable to have lines that sink in order to let the ice float over them. Commercial fishing

chandleries carry a wide range of polypropylene lines. Shore lines can be somewhat smaller than ground tackle if you get out of areas where shock loads from waves or gust are frequent. Lines 3–4 cm thick are adequate for boats up to 50 feet.

▲ High lines. Try to keep the stern line high so that most bergy bits can float under.

On the other hand, if you are wintering the boat in the ice it is important to keep pulling the lines free of the ice, to prevent them being cut or dragging the boat down or around.

When setting up your spider's web of shore lines, speed is of the essence, and having an easy deployment system is essential. If your boat is big enough you can have fancy custom-made stainless steel reels mounted somewhere on deck and they will make both deployment and retrieval quick and easy. Or you can use large mesh bags for deploying your lines, setting them up on the side deck before you reach the anchorage with the line led through large snatch blocks on the stern quarters. This has worked very well for deploying but it took half an hour or so after retrieval to flake all the

▲ Billy Budd using both lines ashore and an anchor in a deep fjord near Uummannaq, West Greenland.

lines back into their bags. Where we could drop the anchor within 500 feet of shore without swinging into anything, we would use a reel of 600 feet of 10 mm line.

We use Spectra as a first line ashore. We winch the boat into place using that line and then replace it with the polypropylene lines at our leisure.

In much of the north, including the Faroes and Iceland, floating ropes can trap ice, which can be useful to protect the boat by keeping ice out, or can be a hazard preventing it from getting out. Sinking ropes do not trap ice but can catch on uneven seabeds. You can also use a metal sinker to weigh down a floating rope, and of course you can use a weight to slide down an anchor chain or line to give a better catanery.

Some recommendations include:
• Rock strops (steel wire loop of 2-metre diameter or so: just a simple loop with the ends fastened together with bulldog clips,

there is no need for fancy spliced wires or mucking about with thimbles and shackles). But long climbing slings can also be used, perhaps doubled up if you are a large boat, or you can attach the main rope directly round the rock if you have enough line.

- Some lengths of steel angle iron for use as giant pitons or for hammering into ice or snow.

A minimum of 100 metres of chain, which allows a 7:1 scope in around 12 m of water, would be great if you have the space and the wallet to match.

- When tying to trees, there is no need for wire or chain; simply tie on with the mooring line, taking an extra turn around the tree before securing. This ensures that the line will not move on the tree, either up or down or back and forth, and eliminates chafe that may damage the tree or the rope.
- Rope bags are the way to go for smaller boats (up to 12 m). It can be a lot easier to put the rope in the dinghy and pay it out that way, and much easier to row that way too.

▼ In deep fjords it is possible to moor the boat directly to the wall using climbing chocks or cams. Here climbers are starting their first ascent of the Impossible Wall, Sortehul, West Greenland, from *Dodo's Delight*.

LINES ASHORE

Lines ashore from the back of the boat and the anchor out front is a combination that works well in secluded anchorages. There are various methods for doing this, but here is one way:

- Use the dinghy to check depth first, spotting any rocks, or use a portable echo sounder if you have one. You are going to back in towards the shore, and running aground going in reverse is something you want to avoid. You might end up damaging the propeller or rudder.
- The dinghy crew should prepare strong holding points for the lines on shore before you start to back in. Use natural attachments such as rocks and trees, but try not to harm them. Wire or chain is best around big objects, and have dedicated systems for hooking them together and for tying in the rope.
- Have designated crew and a firm plan that everybody knows. Here, routine comes into play. Use handheld VHFs and/or agreed signals.
- As the skipper is backing in, the anchor goes off the bow and the dinghy crew starts running lines to the shore.

It can be hard to measure the distance to shore, so a laser rangefinder can come in handy at this point. That way you don't run out of either shore lines or anchor warp before you are firmly secured. But be warned: it is a very expensive piece of kit and you will not use it that often, so maybe it's one for the 'nice to have' list.

Four 100-metre lines are a minimum. Use line that doesn't absorb water as it gets very heavy and if temperatures are below freezing it becomes very hard to handle. The lines can be stored on big rolls. They are very easy to operate, but take up a lot of space. Another solution is webbing on a roll, also known as anchor rolls. They produce a lot of friction at the beginning, so be sure to take out 10–20 metres before you start rowing.

An even more flexible solution is to modify a small spinnaker bag. This is the best solution for boats of 40 feet and under.

◀◀ The views are spectacular from both on and off the boat.

Cut a hole in the bottom of the bag so you can get one end of the rope through. Tie off this end on the boat. The other end of the rope comes out on top, ready to be pulled straight out of the bag. Don't coil the rope in the bag, just stuff it in metre by metre. That way it will not get tangled when you run it ashore. Use a carabiner to attach the bag itself to the guardrail of the boat. Attach the line around your waist and a line from the dinghy – the dinghy's painter perhaps – around your leg. That way you can row to shore and run up to the nearest strong point without getting delayed by securing the dinghy. Be sure to have a long dinghy rope, or painter, or fix a longer line so it doesn't stop you on the way. It is a good idea to practise and refine this technique in good conditions in anchorages where you don't really have to use it, so you are prepared when it gets real. Be sure to dry the bag and rope after use, before storing it. The hole in the bottom helps drain the bag.

▼ Climber's view of 'base camp'!

◀ Shallow water can mean a long dinghy ride. Climbers at the end of the long ski traverse of Northumberland Island.

LEAVING THE BOAT

The main rule here is: don't let everybody go ashore at one and the same time, unless the boat is in sight of someone at all times. There are several examples of eager hikers and sailors who have left their boat at anchor to explore either by dinghy or on foot, with disastrous results. Even if it seems like the anchor has a good hold, the wind may change direction or increase. Katabatic winds (fall winds) may push your boat out of the protected bay while you are miles inland. When you return there is only the dinghy left, and that may have been destroyed by polar bears or even been blown out to sea as well.

If you all have to leave the boat for a short time for some reason, make sure you have at least one line tied to shore. In the high latitudes this means that you have to carry at least one 100-metre line on board. The best is to have at least two or three 100-metre lines so you can run several lines ashore in addition to the anchor.

To be well dressed for the elements is a great boon.

10 CLOTHING

▶Camping on the beach, suitably clothed at the end of Northumberland Island, ski traverse.

There are two types of clothing you might need in the high latitudes: hiking clothes and sailing clothes. After a number of years doing both activities in high latitudes, I have come to the conclusion that hiking outdoor clothes are the right type for me, both on and off the water.

There are two reasons for this. First of all, it is more practical to have one main set of outdoor clothes, and second, today's clothing technology is really outstanding. Therefore, in most conditions that do not involve heavy rain or sea spray I use standard GORE-TEX jackets and trousers. If the weather gets really nasty, I have a waterproof coat with a big hood and an insulating layer to keep me warm when I go outside. The few times I have to go on deck, it will do the trick. But be aware of the difference between standard GORE-TEX trousers and salopettes. You will end up wet sitting on deck if you don't wear salopettes, as the water more often than not will find its way down into regular-cut rain trousers.

The same goes for the three-layer principle: during physical activity we produce surplus heat and our body regulates its temperature by perspiring. When the perspiration evaporates, the body temperature cools down. Where our clothing does not allow the perspiration to evaporate, there is hardly any cooling possible. Therefore, the layer closest to the skin must allow perspiration to evaporate. If it does not, the perspiration will create an uncomfortable damp feeling, and in extreme cold this could even be dangerous. The second layer acts as an insulation layer. The third layer is the protection against the elements. However, the perspiration must still be allowed to pass from the inner layer though the next layers to the outside. The thinner the three layers, the more precise the regulation. If all layers are properly coordinated, they can work interactively with each other.

- Close to the body: do not wear cotton as it retains sweat and never dries properly. Use wool, and preferably merino wool. The colder it is, the more layers you can add. Many thin layers are better than one thick one as it is easier to regulate the temperature, and the layers provide insulation in themselves.

◄ The crew on *RX II* Finn Andreassen, skipper Trond Aasvoll, and Hans Fredrik Haukeland tied up to an ice floe and properly dressed.

- Mid layer: use wool or fleece.
- Protection: water and wind resistant, with a hood and high collar. It is better to have an oversized jacket/coat than one with a tight fit, as the extra air provides additional insulation.

Using this layering principle, items made by well-known and reputable companies such as Patagonia, The North Face, Rab and several others work very well in high latitudes.

On my feet I prefer thick-soled sailing or fishing boots, or boots with furry linings built in. The stuff you get in the serious fishing or workmen shops are not necessarily the smartest, but they do the job. Remember that fishermen are out in freezing cold nights on a daily basis and years of experience have taught them what to wear – and what not to wear.

So, boots – some of the warmest we have used are Dunlop Purofort Thermo Kings, although the soles are a bit thick and clumsy. Muck Boots, from Canada, are good – not as warm but more comfortable, and you can hike in them. People working in extreme cold, such as snowmobile drivers in the high north, are the right kind of people to ask for advice when it comes to both gloves and boots.

Fishermen also know what to wear on their hands. Forget expensive GORE-TEX gloves – as soon as you start handling long

► Even the chef uses wool as the first and second layer to keep warm.

◀ High neck. Fleece with hoods and high neck is very welcome for those cold days.

lines soaked with ice-cold water, they get wet. The same goes for when you have to remove tons of kelp from your anchor, hanging off the bow. Cold hands are a real pain. Get yourself a couple of pairs (no need to save a few bucks here) of solid rubber gloves. Buy the ones without a liner. The liner will get wet and the process of drying them will take longer. Use fleece or wool inner gloves, and have three or four pairs so you can have a pair drying out while one keeps you warm. But having said that, rubber gloves with a 'fur' lining are a great and simple comfort if you can keep them dry inside – or buy two pairs.

Have at least three warm, windproof hats; you'll probably lose one over the side, and the other two can be rotated, one wet, one drying.

Finally, ski goggles. You won't look very 'yachty', but when heavy cold rain or snow is blowing horizontally right in your face, you won't worry about looks – just comfort and the ability to actually see where you are sailing.

Glacial silt can provide depth for anchoring, amidst staggering scenery.

11 SAILING AREAS

▲ Svalbard is the most accessible polar area for sailors and offers midnight sun.

The iconic high latitude sailor H. W. 'Bill' Tilman started sailing to Patagonia after his days as a pure mountain climber were over. He wanted to combine the adventures of sailing and climbing, there in the south. He found the adventures he wanted, but as he was living in England he started to look for areas closer to home. He found Greenland. He continued to sail and climb until he disappeared in a fierce storm off the Falklands in 1977, at the age of 79. He was on his way to yet another climbing expedition in the south.

This goes to show that many of us can sail towards new adventures in the high latitudes at any age – and that we have areas worth spending a lifetime in just a few weeks' sailing away. Here is a rough guide to the high latitude areas.

SVALBARD

Svalbard is a very accessible wilderness where you can explore both your own boundaries and its nature. In fact it is the high latitude area most easily reached. From Tromsø to Svalbard on your own keel takes around 3 days, and puts you right among icebergs, glaciers, polar bears and wildlife. Some miles further north you reach the pack ice, and you have to walk the rest of the way to the North Pole.

As a sailor you have to apply for a cruising permit if you are going to Svalbard on your own boat. It is recommended that you have an AIS receiver and transmitter, a VHF-radio (25 W), an Iridium telephone, proper survival suits and a liferaft. You must have a rifle and know how to use it. Weapons can be rented in Longyearbyen.

The Svalbard Treaty gives you as a sailor the right to sail in the area as long as you comply with the rules and regulations set by Norway. It is very rare, if ever, that Sysselmannen declines an application for a sailing permit, as long as you have done what you have to, and have the necessary sailing experience. It is, as always, good to seek information and advice from sailors who have experience in the area.

Contact Sysselmannen well in advance of your expedition on firmapost@sysselmannen.no and familiarise yourself with local regulations, particularly those dealing with environmental and safety precautions.

Svalbard has a polar climate and you must expect temperatures between 0 and 10°C in the summer time. If you venture into the far north, into Hinlopen or east of Nordaustlandet, expect colder temperatures, as the water from the polar basin comes in to play instead of the Gulf Stream.

The prevailing winds in summer are generally light and variable, so make sure to stock up on diesel.

Arctic fog is frequent in the summer, as the mild air from the south comes in contact with the cold water surface. But as a general rule, with ice the fog is often low-lying and if you get up the mast, you can get above the fog.

The best time to enter Hinlopen or Nordauslandet is from mid-August to the end of September. But this is also the time

▼ Barentsburg offers a glimpse of the arctic Russian society.

when the weather gets more unsettled and you risk heavier weather. The sun also goes below the horizon.

When you sail east of Verlegenhuken – the most northerly point of Spitsbergen – you must keep a very keen eye on the weather and the weather forecast. Download ice charts via Iridium, or have a person on land watching the charts and sending you satellite SMS warnings. If a strong northerly or north-easterly wind sets in, it can be a matter of hours before the ice reaches land and you are at risk of being trapped. If you are in Hinlopen the ice can actually close you in as it comes drifting on both sides of Nordaustlandet. If you are on the north side of Nordaustlandet you also risk being trapped.

Calving glacier fronts can be very dangerous as there is no telling when an ice block might fall. A distance of 200 metres is a reasonable minimum to avoid falling ice and big waves. If the fjord is narrow and the ice front higher than 40–50 metres, it is advisable to keep further away than 200 metres.

See www.sysselmannen.no for more information.

‖ ▼ Clyde River, East Baffin.

■ CANADA

▲ Anchored off Pond Inlet, Baffin. An open roadstead; care and a watch are needed.

Baffin Island has mostly easterly winds, and the cold current flowing south brings fog and ice to the area. The best time to sail here is mid-July to mid-August since the light will be fading fast the later you go, and ice and darkness is not the best mix in the world. But often the ice is slow to clear from the east Baffin shore. The Northwest Passage through Canada is a story of its own – see the next chapter.

GREENLAND

The weather on the west coast is mostly stable and good. The farther north you get the more stable and good it can be. It is much the same as with the high pressure system over the Antarctic peninsular.

The best time to sail in Greenland is early July to August or into September, due to the ice conditions. It can be earlier still up to about the Disko Bay area. Generally speaking, going further north it is a case of the later the better from the ice point of view. Earlier approaches close to the south coast can be blocked by storis, the arctic ice travelling down the east coast and round to the west coast. Even later approaches here can be stopped by ice, although it usually clears in the later months of the summer.

But you also have to consider your return trip. If you don't plan to overwinter your boat in Greenland, or Iceland, which can be a good alternative, you will have to deal with dark nights and the possibility of an autumn Atlantic gale or two if you leave your return till September or even October. That might not be the best ending for a high latitude cruise, but it gives you more time in Greenland, and provides a challenge.

◀◀ Kangersuatsiaq (Prøven) the most picturesque settlement on the west coast of Greenland?

Cape Farvel can be a crux. This is the Cape Horn of the Arctic, and you basically have two options. One is to take the inland route of Prinz Christian Sund, ice permitting, which is very scenic and has a lot of mountains and walls you could climb. The Weather Station on the east side used to be a popular stop for most sailors, with some tricky pilotage into the small harbour but Danish pastries at the end if you were lucky. However, it is no longer permanently manned.

The other option is to avoid it altogether and go round to the south, but then you should leave *at least* 100 nautical miles between you and the cape. The weather can be violent and combined with the current that runs south along the east coast and pushes the storis (pack ice) and ice bergs the same way, it can create pretty nasty conditions in the area.

Reporting

Vessels over 20 gross register tonnage in an area 200 nautical miles around Greenland have to send Position Reports to the Danish Navy at MRCC Nuuk. This can be done by phone, satellite telephone or email, and has to be done every 6th hour.

Smaller vessels may also use this system in order to be more visible to the authorities. But be aware that when you decide to join the reporting system you have to report at the times specified. If you fail to report, a SAR operation will soon be launched, and you might be held economically responsible if you trigger a false SAR operation.

When you get close to the coast you can switch to report to Aasiaat Radio via VHF. The routine is to inform them of your daily sailing plan; when in harbour/at anchor send in a new report. You must also report deviations from your plan. To date this is not obligatory for small non-commercial boats.

The entire Greenlandic coast is coordinated by Aasiaat Radio. All other stations are used as relay and not manned.

You can find the full regulations and information here, and please take the time to study them carefully:

GREENPOS message content:

System identifier: GREENPOS
A – Ship's name and call sign
B – Date Time Group (UTC)
C or D – Position
E – True course
F – Speed

I – Destination and ETA (UTC)
L – Intended voyage
Q – Defects and deficiencies
S – Weather and ice conditions
X – Total number of persons on board and other relevant information

MRCC Nuuk numbers
Inmarsat: C: 433 116 710
Email: ako-commcen@mil.dk

Phone: +299 364023
Fax: +299 364099

System identifier: COASTAL CONTROL
A – Ship's name and call sign
B – Date Time Group (LT)
C or D – Position
E – True course
F – Speed

I – Destination and ETA (LT)
L – Intended voyage
Q – Defects and deficiencies
X – Total number of persons on board and other relevant information

Aasiaat Radio
MMSI: 003313000
Email: OYR@TELEPOST.GL

Phone: +299 386 993
Phone: +299 130 000
Fax: +299 892 777

ICELAND

Iceland consists of one main island and numerous smaller ones. A passage to Iceland and a cruise along its rugged coasts during its short summer, offers an experience difficult to match anywhere else in the North Atlantic.

Although there are not many local yachts, repair facilities are relatively good, particularly in active fishing harbours such as Reykjavik, Isafjördur and Olafsvik. Reykjavik and Keflavik are the most frequented in Iceland, although visiting yachts are relatively few in number.

The Vestmannaeyjar Islands in the south are also well worth a visit.

In spite of Iceland's proximity to the Arctic Circle, the climate is not too harsh and winters are relatively mild, mainly because of the warming waters of the Gulf Stream. The average temperatures are 10°C in summer and 1°C in winter. Prevailing winds are from the SE or E. Summer winds are often light and calms are common.

▲ Nuuk, capital of West Greenland, can be crowded.

CAPE HORN

If you dream of high latitude sailing, then Cape Horn stands out as one of the real landmarks for making a toast as you sail past. Rounding the Horn, under sail, on a non-stop passage of more than 3,000 miles passing through the latitude of 50 degrees south both east and west of Cape Horn, renders sailors eligible to apply for membership of the exclusive International Association of Cape Horners: an organisation whose origins lie among those who rounded the Horn as professional seamen serving upon the tall ships of the Clipper era. There are no exceptions to the association's strict joining criteria, whose membership now includes members of crews from several notable Round the World Yacht races and others in small boats who have shared the same unique experience – the 'Mount Everest' of ocean sailing.

The main season is December to April, and usual starting points for sailing round the island of the Horn rather than a true 'Rounding of the Horn', as above, are Puerto Williams or Ushuaia, the Falkland Islands, or even Antarctica.

ANTARCTICA

It is roughly 600 nautical miles from Cape Horn to the South Shetland Islands just north of the Antarctic Peninsula. You can expect at least one gale during the crossing, as the low-pressure systems push through the Drake Passage every third day as a general rule. There is also a good chance that you will end up in the middle of a low. The wind will decrease significantly. But even if it feels a little too laid back, don't bother to shake out those reefs. It's only a brief lull, with 2–3 hours of relief. Then it will start blowing hard again, perhaps from a different direction.

Be sure to follow the weather closely before departure, and if you think about getting external help from a weather router – do so. They will most likely contribute to making your crossing, both ways, more comfortable and safe. There is a list of weather routers in Chapter 8.

Equipment for Antarctica

A voyage to the Antarctic Peninsula from Tierra del Fuego is likely to be of long duration for a small boat – you must carry supplies for at least 8 weeks, as it is not unknown for smaller private yachts to wait for up to six weeks for a weather window to return north. You cannot resupply anywhere in Antarctica, period! So if you want a supply drop there, you must make your own arrangements with a national authority, expedition support specialist company or a cruise ship operator, at considerable cost.

▲ Lemaire Channel. Squeezing through the narrow gap between a big grounded iceberg and the cliff at the southern end.

A good buy before leaving for Antarctica is *A Complete Guide to Antarctic Wildlife* by Hadoram Shirihai.

General information for sailing to Antarctica is available from the IAATO website, specifically the yacht outreach pamphlet. See here for more information: www.iaato.org/home

Antarctica permits must be sought from the flag state of your yacht or expedition. There are no exceptions: a permit is

Sabbath rest in Dorian Bay,
Antarctica.

SOUTH GEORGIA

South Georgia is regarded by many high latitude sailors as their favourite place. It's utterly remote: 800 nautical miles from the Falkland Islands and 2,600 nautical miles from the Cape of Good Hope. The scenery is just outstanding, with glaciers, snow-covered peaks stretching up almost 3,000 metres, and incredible wildlife.

Captain James Cook circumnavigated the island in 1775 and made the first landing. He claimed the territory for the United Kingdom, and it is still a British overseas territory today. The island has a rich history of whaling. The Norwegians ran large whaling operations out of stations such as Grytviken, and hunted certain whale species to near extinction. Ernest Shackleton's epic sail from Elephant Island, Antarctica, to the south-west coast of South Georgia on a rescue mission in a small boat in 1916 is also part of the island's unique history. Shackleton died there in 1922 on another expedition, and is buried in Grytviken.

South Georgia is 167 kilometres long and between 1.4 and 37 kilometres wide. The side that faces south-west is constantly battered by waves from the depressions that rotate around Antarctica. All the settlements are on the north-east side.

◀◀ Walrus colony at Devon Island. Looked like rocks when we anchored, till they moved!

The combination of high mountains, glaciers and fjords on the north-east side makes for a dangerous breeding place for williwaws. When the heavy, dense air meets the mountains' west side, it is forced up along the mountainsides and over the top, and increases in speed as it plummets down the other side. If you feel a sudden rush of warm air or see a crater in the sea near the shore, expect big gusts – in South Georgia they can reach up to 100 knots.

Typical daily maximum temperatures in South Georgia at sea level are around 0°C in winter (August) and 8°C in summer (January). Winter minimum temperatures are typically about −5°C and rarely dip below −10°C. Annual precipitation in South Georgia is about 1,500mm, much of which falls as sleet or snow, which is possible in any month. Inland, the snow line in summer is at an altitude of about 300 metres.

Charter yacht visits usually start in the Falkland Islands, last between four and six weeks, and enable guests to visit the remote harbours of South Georgia and the South Sandwich Islands. Sailing vessels are now required to anchor off and can no longer tie up to the old whaling piers on shore, as the station's infrastructure is rapidly disintegrating, and it can be dangerous. One exception to this is the recently upgraded yacht berth at Grytviken. All other jetties at former whaling stations lie inside a 200-metre exclusion zone, and berthing, or running ropes ashore, at these places is forbidden. When visiting South Georgia, yachts are normally expected to report to the Government Officer at King Edward Point before moving round the island.

Here you will find all the applications and documents you need to fill out: http://www.gov.gs/

Check here for the latest weather forecast: http://www.weather-forecast.com/maps/South-Georgia-and-the-South-Sandwich-Islands

See also Chapter 14: South Georgia.

■ PATAGONIA

▶▶ Ushuaia is a beautiful place to anchor.

The Argentine climate ranges from subtropical in the north to cold temperate in Tierra del Fuego. The central zone is temperate, while Buenos Aires is hot and humid, the summer months December to February being the hottest. In Rio de la Plata the prevailing winds in summer are easterly, while SW winds are more common in winter. They are often accompanied by pamperos, violent SW squalls that affect most of Argentina's coastal waters.

There aren't many boats sailing in the Patagonian archipelago, and you can go for days without seeing anything else other than local wildlife and snow-capped mountains and glaciers. You must report your position regularly to the Chilean authorities to comply with the local rules. *Patagonia and Tierra Del Fuego Nautical Guide* by Mariolina Rolfo and Giorgio Ardrizz is a must-have for any sailor visiting this region.

Boats moored at jetty, Cambridge Bay.

12

THE NORTHWEST PASSAGE

by Trond Aasvoll

AN ARCTIC CIRCUMNAVIGATION

Norwegians have a long and proud track record for sailing in cold waters. In 2009 and 2010 Trond Aasvoll and his crew on the 36-foot American fibreglass boat *RX II* established a new record by becoming the first Norwegians to circum-navigate the North Pole. Here is an account of Aasvoll's hard-earned experiences.

◀◀ Italian, French and British boats at the jetty at Tuktoyaktuk.

Boat stats

Name: *RX II*

Builder: Designed by Jerry Cartwright, built at Oddington Yachts, Newport

Launched: 1977

Material: Fibreglass

Displacement: approx. 9,000 kg

Length: 10.97 metres LOA

Beam: 3.08 metres

Draught: 1.7 metres

Propulsion: Volvo 2030 engine, 30 hp

Crew: 3

As with most expeditions, it started with a temptation that a restless soul couldn't resist. No one had ever sailed round the North Pole in one single season. The ever-increasing temperature had, sadly enough, made both the Northeast and Northwest Passage open for smaller yachts. Several leisure boats had sailed one or the other of the famous passages, but no one had done both in one season. So, 'why not?' I thought, and I started to look for suitable crew.

It is no easy feat to find crews for such a hard voyage: ice, fog, remoteness, insecurity, polar bears, storms, living in close quarters for months on end, and with rough sailing at the best of times. Knowledge on how to sail a boat was not necessarily the deciding factor. The ability to adapt, improvise and have physical stamina would be far more important. And most of all we had to get along together and work as a team when the days became long, wet and windy. That was an absolute requirement if the expedition was to be successful.

I eventually managed to get hold of Hans Fredrik Haukeland, who is a quiet and cool-headed man in all situations. No wonder, as his occupation was a fire-fighter – and he

◀◀ Sixty per cent more ice in the Arctic in 2013, compared to 2012.

could sail and knew his way around an engine. His training as a fire-fighter included first aid, so he instantly became the ship's pharmacist and doctor.

Finn Andreassen was the youth on board, and he had just finished his agricultural education. He was the most feisty, so he could be sent up the mast in a hurry when needed. He was a competent sailor with experience of ocean sailing. He became our electronics expert and took care of both the software and hardware on board.

I took on the role of skipper and expedition leader. All my experience gained from short-handed and solo sailing in Scandinavia and Europe, two eastward Atlantic crossings and a lot of sailing in the Mediterranean would come in handy. I hold a D5L recreational skipper certificate and also a light aircraft certificate. So my responsibilities became weather, ice maps, navigation through the ice and making sure the boat maintained an average speed of 4.5 knots during the passage. That was the speed we needed to average in order to get through in time.

My only high latitude sailing experience at that point had been a February solo sail from Arendal to Bodø, above the Arctic Circle.

The three sailors set out on 29 June from Arendal on the south coast of Norway. Next stop Vardø, close to the Russian border. That's 1,100 nautical miles as the crow flies just to get to the starting point.

Statistically, the Northeast Passage opens on 12 August (2009) and the Northwest Passage closes on 24 September. That allows 45 days to cover the 3,125 nautical mile circumnavigation of the North Pole. RX II isn't a fast boat, but we reckoned she would manage 100 nautical miles on average every day.

It was just about right. We used 29 days from Vardø to the Bering Strait. It was a cold experience. For heating inside the RX II, we had a pot-burner type 3kW Refleks oven and a 3.5kW Eberspächer air heater – both diesel burners. They were very useful when the days were cold, stressful and wet.

We knew no one with experience to tell us about the ice and conditions we could expect: when the ice would open, where the current would be favourable, where it would be deep enough to sail, and when and where it would be best to stop for a power nap. And not least, how to navigate in dense fog, dense ice, and where the compass is totally useless. After all, our main goal was to sail through all of this with a 36-foot fibreglass sailboat with a small 30hp diesel engine – and live to tell the tale.

▼ When sailing in cold climates, meat is best kept hanging in the rigging where sun, wind and salt can preserve it.

▶▶ Lots of on-board storage space is a huge advantage when spending weeks at sea.

▼ Deep freeze in tunnels 10 metres down in permafrost in Tuktoyaktuk.

The wildlife was spectacular, and we had encounters with birds, polar bears, walruses and seals every day. But that's not the only thing we had encounters with. The Russians were on our tail and did not accept the clearance papers we had received from the government before leaving. This forced us to sail to Providenia, and thereby effectively ended our attempt to sail both passages in one season. While the bureaucracy ground away, the ice in the Northwest Passage went and came. We were disappointed to the point of tears and had to leave *RX II* in Nome for the winter. We would have to wait, and only return the following spring.

Food

Based on our experience travelling the Northeast Passage the year before, we opted for a whole reindeer, salted and dried, as

our main meat source. Was this a powerful and nutritious diet? Sailing in cold weather requires a lot of calories.

We supplemented this with long-life milk, bread, eggs, bacon, beans, butter, margarine, coffee and cocoa, among other things.

When the weather got really bad, we stuck to the Norwegian high-tech dried meals from Real Turmat. Just add boiling water and you have a nutritious and tasty meal five minutes later. In storm conditions we added more water so that it all turned into soup – much easier to just drink the whole meal straight from the bag instead of fiddling around with cutlery. One hand for the meal, and one hand for the boat.

Navigation and safety equipment

We had watertight 120-litre grab bags containing tents, clothing, cooking equipment, miscellaneous items and Real Turmat for 40 days. This was in case we had to leave the boat in an emergency.

We used a SPOT Satellite GPS Messenger to give our shore crew back home our position and to let them know that everything was OK. This, or the inReach, is a great boon to have, and it also covers rescue insurance through the monthly subscription. Our Iridium satellite phone was used to download GRIB files (see Chapter 8, Weather, for an updated list of web services) and ice charts from NSIDC-AMSR-E satellite and from the Canadian Ice Service.

THE NUMBERS

I calculated that 900 litres of diesel for the two heaters and some motoring in the light airs would be sufficient to reach Cambridge Bay, Canada. Here we could refuel.

◀ 'Sword of Damocles' of ice blocking exit from Prince Regent Inlet, 2013.

We used 587 litres of diesel from Nome to Cambridge Bay, a distance of 1,771 nautical miles.

- We left Nome on 31 July and arrived at Point Barrow on 4 August.
- We left Pauline Cove, Herschel Island on 7 August, and arrived at Booth Island on 11 August, then Cambridge Bay on 16 August.

That's 17 days of sailing, including the pit stop.

For the 584 nautical miles from Clyde River to Nuuk, we used 100 litres of diesel.

- We left Clyde River on 31 August and arrived at Nuuk on 4 September.

Total distance Northwest Passage: 3,817 nautical miles. A total of 36 days.

For the next 1,462 nautical miles, which took us from Cambridge Bay to Clyde River, we used 570 litres of diesel.

- We left Cambridge Bay on 19 August and arrived at Bellot Strait on 24 August.
- We left Barrow Strait/Lancaster Sound on 25 August and arrived at Clyde River on 30 August.

For the 2,040 nautical miles from Nuuk to Arendal, we used 560 litres of diesel.

- We left Nuuk on 7 September and arrived in Norway on 29 September, then home in Arendal on 9 October.

The total distance was 5,857 nautical miles. Overall, 61 days to Norway.

Fuel consumption was roughly 1.7–2.4 litres per hour for heating, engine operating and charging current.

▲ In Bellot Strait, 2013.

We sent the U.S. Coast Guard our sailing plan in Alaskan waters and made sure to check in and out of Canada. The Canadian Coast Guard keeps a helpful service and lookout in its waters, so it is a good thing to keep them informed as they can provide ice information and possible assistance if needed.

It is very important to have shore crew on such expeditions. We had Jon Amtrup, Lars Ingeberg, Vincent Frigstad and Knut Espen Solberg standing by at all times with advice and information. Each one has their special field of knowledge concerning ice in the Arctic, weather, locations, media, shipping and coordination of bits and bobs. A number of times it paid off to have someone to gather information and with whom we could then discuss things so we could choose the right course – when to sail and when to wait for the ice up ahead to clear, or just to have another person to talk to apart from the other two on board.

▼ *Dodo's Delight* at start of Bellot Strait, 2013.

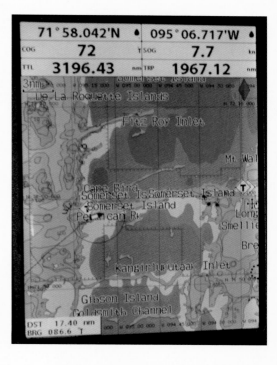

▲ The Panasonic Toughbook with internal GPS and charts is a handy back-up plotter.

After having been awake for two days sailing in difficult conditions in ice, gales and fog, we needed someone else to get our heads straight and to help us make the right decisions. Sometimes we were completely worn out, both physically and mentally. But that's part of the adventure, and when getting out on the right side is the result, it is all worthwhile.

For navigation we used two Panasonic CF-29 Toughbook laptops with built-in GPS. They are waterproof and shockproof, and a must when sailing in a boat with an open cockpit. They functioned without a glitch on both passages. See www.custom-toughbooks.com for information.

◄◄ *Dodo's Delight's* transits of the Northwest Passage. **Top**: East-west, 2012, via Peel Sound; **bottom**: West-east, 2013, via Bellot Strait.

The compass was completely useless in certain areas of the Northwest Passage due to massive magnetic variation. We therefore programmed the internal GPS unit to update the position every third second, so when we sailed at 1 knot or less in thick fog without any steering reference, we could see where we were at all times on the screen. The variation also rendered the autopilot useless, as from time to time it took us on a 360-degree turn, then a 90-degree turn and so on. The only solution was either hand steering or to let the autopilot steer to a waypoint.

Close passage

After leaving Nome in July 2010 with a heavily loaded boat, life was good and we enjoyed the lovely sight of the sea and Alaskan nature. But life changes quickly in the high north. The wind increased to storm force and we had a countercurrent kicking up a nasty sea. Just to add to the mayhem, we also encountered ice.

The wind had pushed the ice all the way to the coast and, according to the ice charts, had also filled from Point Barrow to the Canadian border. As we sailed into the ice, the wind dropped and the fog came rolling in with a slight breeze from the east. Eventually, the ice became too dense to sail through. We had to get out. Ice charts showed little or no ice close to the coast. It was our only chance, and we went for it. The chart was quite right: the big ice had run aground in 4–10 metres of water, so we sailed along the inside edge of the ice in 3 metres of depth, all the way east to the Canada border.

We arrived in Cambridge Bay on 16 August. This was also the date when, statistically, the Northwest Passage had opened in the last

▲ It was colder in the Northwest Passage in 2013, compared to 2012. Spray turned to ice on contact, Lancaster Sound, 2013.

few years, so we were on schedule. There was still a lot of ice west and east of King William Island and even in the Bellot Strait, so we had to wait a few days.

Here we met the legendary Peter Semotiuk, the man who helps sailors with weather reports worldwide over the SSB radio. He gave us a great welcome and it was fun to meet him at last. Many sailors have talked to him over the ham net, but very few who have benefited from his excellent service have ever had the opportunity to meet him in person. Peter told us that we were the first boat to reach Cambridge Bay that year.

Here we resupplied the *RX II* with diesel, gas and food before we set off on 19 August through the Queen Maud Gulf. We were blessed with fair weather but almost no wind. In the James Ross Strait we had to be extra careful with our navigation. Here, Roald Amundsen ran aground with Gjøa and got stuck in gale force winds. He had to throw everything that could be thought of as unnecessary overboard in order to lighten the ship, to get her afloat again.

Amundsen's groundbreaking voyage must have been a totally different and far more challenging experience than our expedition. We had half-decent maps and GPS, while he had no maps and a compass that was totally useless because of the huge (often 35–50-degree) magnetic variation in the area.

This is what we wrote in the log book in the coming days:

■ 22 August

We have been informed that Bellot Strait is packed full and completely clogged with ice. Franklin Strait and Peel Sound is open up to Barrow Strait and Lancaster Sound!

■ 23 August

James Ross Strait is behind us now. Compass and autopilot on a magnetic compass course go completely crazy because of the variation. On Tasmania Island, we meet the Swedish yacht *Ariel 4* sailing west and a few hours later the Swedish ship *Anna* and the Polish ship *Solanas*. All well: wind and sun.

■ 25 August

Entered the north of Parry Channel, 74°12'N 93°25'W and sailed east into Lancaster Sound. 1.5°C, fog, sun shines through the fog, icebergs.

The wind freshens the following days with easterly and north-easterly winds, and it is very cold. We choose to go north and east of Bylot Island, because there is a lot of ice in Eclipse Sound. We are still struggling with the compass heading on the autopilot and must use 'course to waypoint'.

■ 30 August

Arrived Clyde River. There have been a lot of icebergs along the way, so we had to keep a constant lookout. This is very tiresome with only three people on board as only one can rest at a time. As we head further south the nights get darker, and this makes the sailing even more challenging. Crossing from Clyde River to Nuuk, we got gale force winds from the north and much ice in Baffin Bay.

■ 4 September

Arrived Nuuk. Northwest Passage done without problems with a 36-foot fibreglass boat with an open cockpit and a crew of three. Very happy.

We sailed the last part back to Norway with only two on board and had the not-so-good experiences of breaking the boom at Cape Farewell, the autopilot breaking down, an unreliable engine, and two big storms.

We were totally exhausted, both mentally and physically, on our return and had to spend a whole week in bed. But of course, it was all worth it.

Expedition leader and captain of the
RX II
Trond A. Aasvoll
4815 Saltrød
Email: trond.aasvool@online.no
Tel: +47 97548623

ⓘ **Please note:** At the time of going to print, some experienced arctic sailors had begun discussions towards forming a Voluntary Codes of Practice for arctic sailing, in an attempt to forestall or amend more onerous regulations from national and international regulatory boards. The discussions were only at the formative stage at this point, but it would be well for any intending arctic sailing to check on this first.

You will sail past abandoned villages in the Northeast Passage.

13

THE NORTHEAST PASSAGE

by Elena Solovyeva

THE BEAUTY AND CHALLENGES OF SAILING IN RUSSIA

Sailing in Russia is no walk in the park for foreigners, as several explorers have discovered. But there is help to be found, and it is highly advisable to get a local expert to guide you through the paperwork and people, institutions and bureaucracy that exist. Here Elena Solovyeva, CEO of Russian Passage and high latitude sailor, shares her knowledge.

Sailing on the Russian north coast is regulated by different laws of the Russian Federation and requires special permits. The number of permits depends on the route you choose, and the places and ports of call you are planning to visit. Calling at ports closed to foreign vessels, or visits to the territories of national parks or areas with special boundary regimes, requires you to apply for additional papers.

The most popular routes and destinations for sailors are Franz Josef Land, Novaya Zemlya and the Northeast Passage.

The most beautiful cruising ground is the Franz Josef Land archipelago. There are many glaciers and icebergs, and a variety of animals

▼ Wildlife. Arctic terns are beautiful and aggressive when you get in to their territories.

◀◀ Reindeer antlers left to dry.

including polar bears, seals, walruses and whales. Also, if you are fond of the history of exploration in high latitudes, you will find it interesting to visit the points from where the great expeditions started, the places where they wintered, and Soviet polar stations preserved to the present day.

Novaya Zemlya is closer to the mainland, but you will be able to visit only the northern part: Cape Zhelaniya and Russian Bay. The rest of the archipelago's territory is closed by the military. It is not as impressive as Franz Josef Land, but is still very beautiful with its glaciers.

Both Franz Josef Land and the northern part of Novaya Zemlya are national parks, so you have to comply with the national rules. Probably one of the most inconvenient for sailors is that you must have a national park ranger on board during your stay in the territory of the national park.

The Northeast Passage lies between the Novaya Zemlya archipelago and Cape Dezhnev. The special Northeast Passage service regulates sailing on this route. After they receive the set of documents for your boat, they will give their recommendations for the voyage. You can be recommended to have an ice pilot on board, or to follow an icebreaker on some parts of the route, but the usual requirement for sailing yachts is to stay in areas of ice-free water. Mostly these terms

depend on the ice conditions that season. You can also be ordered to have a technical inspection in one of the Russian ports before the Northeast Passage. Special equipment, like drysuits, should be on board.

Communication is very important. You must have a satellite phone on board as you will have to send your position reports to different services. The same goes for sailing to Franz Josef Land or Novaya Zemlya.

The best time to sail in the Russian north is from the middle of July to the middle of September. Ice conditions are not good for yachts before this period and the storm season starts in late September. If you are thinking about sailing the Northeast Passage and the Northwest Passage in one season, you should start your voyage in the middle of July. The most complicated parts on the Northeast Passage are near the Taimyr Peninsula and Ayon Island, where the Taimyr and Ayon ice massifs cause trouble not only for sailing yachts, but even for big ships and icebreakers.

If you are planning to sail only the Northeast Passage and you don't have to hurry, you can start your voyage in August. The ice conditions of the last few years indicate that this is a good time for sailing there on a yacht.

Those who are planning to pass over both Russia and Canada have two options: sail straight from Murmansk to Alaska, or sail

▶ Weather-torn landscape.

along the Russian coast with the possibility of entering Russian ports. The first option is much faster, but you have to be sure that you have enough diesel, water and food so you won't have to enter any port. Almost all of them are closed to foreign vessels, so a special permit for entering is required. Of course you can call at ports in case of emergency, but you will have to prove that you actually have a life-and-death situation on your hands. If you fail to do that you will pay a fee and lose visa rights to enter Russia for five years. Being out of food, water or diesel is not a valid reason as far as Russian border services are concerned – that is just a matter of bad planning. If you get into such a situation, you have to inform the border services in your daily reports and ask for a permit to enter the nearest port.

The second possibility takes more time because you will have to sail to Providenia to pass border and customs controls. But the advantage is that if you have the permits to enter Russian ports for the entire trip, and you can refuel and replenish supplies and meet up with the local communities.

So, as you can see, the expedition has to be well planned. And timing is very important: the set of documents for the permits should be sent six months before the expeditions. Otherwise, the officials can refuse to give you the permit because the application was sent in too late. We would advise you to start planning the route earlier as there are a lot of things that have to be decided: whether or not you will make stops or not, will you need to call at ports for refuelling and so on.

Elena Solovyeva
Email: elena_soloveva@list.ru
Tel: +7 909 577 08 15

Novara anchored in the
beautiful St. Andrew's Bay.

14

SOUTH GEORGIA

by Bob Shepton

Prince Olav
Harbour
Elsehul
Possession Bay
Stromness
Grytviken
Ocean Harbour
St. Andrews Bay
Gold Harbour
Iris Bay
Wirik
Salomon Glacier
Larsen

SAILING SOUTH GEORGIA

South Georgia is a superb place, full of interest, challenge and adventure. It is true that it is hedged about, as is Antarctica, with a multitude of regulations, but if you start negotiations early and have the budget available for such things as the permit, it is still possible for a private yacht to go there. It is well worth the effort.

Boat stats

Name: *Novara*

Manufacturer: Damstra, Holland

Launched: 1997

Material: Aluminium

Rig: Aero-rigged centre board schooner

Length: 18.3 metres

Beam: 1.7 metres

Beam: 4.5 metres

Draught: 3.1 metres

Propulsion: Perkins Sabre M135, 135hp diesel

Crew: usually 3 or 4

▼ A sleeping elephant seal. They can be found all over the islands.

◄◄ *Novara* anchored in the beautiful Wirik Bay.

Our skipper, Steve Brown, having gained the necessary permits and permissions for our passage from Port Stanley in the Falklands to Grytviken, South Georgia, took just five days and eight hours. It broke all the rules, or at least expectations. Here we were in the Scotia Sea at the eastern end of Drake Passage, one of the stormiest seas in the world, and we had balmy breezes of force 4 or 5, occasionally 6, broad or beam reaching our way across. Perhaps the weather was protesting at the effrontery of our using such a powerful boat, a 60-foot aero-rigged schooner with unstayed masts and booms revolving as integral units, with a foresail and main on each mast and boom. We were

able then to catch the breeze with its two full sail areas.

It is necessary to make Grytviken your first port of call in order to check in properly to South Georgia. The Government Officer Paula was entirely welcoming, at the same time giving us an efficient and effective briefing

▲ Grytviken should be your first port of call when visiting South Georgia.

on the regulations – and finding Scottish grass seeds in the turn-ups of my waterproof trousers! We were introduced to the practice of stepping into disinfectant as we left the boat and again as we returned, and of checking our clothing to make sure we were not guilty of cross-fertilisation from one area to another. South Georgia is a World Heritage Site and they are rightly concerned to keep it pristine and original.

We spent a week in Grytviken waiting for weather and so enjoyed the industrial archaeology of the old whaling station, and the museum, with its shed next door. Within the latter was a replica of Shackleton's small boat, and the minimalist gear for his famous

traverse, after the epic 650-mile passage in the *James Caird* from Elephant Island. Grytviken is the only whaling station where you can still walk around freely as the others are in dangerous states of disintegration and have a 200-metre 'keep out' zone. Paula and the BAS scientists even had us to drinks and dinner, but I was ordered by the skipper then to repay them with slide shows of past expeditions! We then embarked on a harbour-hopping campaign down the north and north-east coast of the island, and in fact by the end of the trip had navigated the whole of the island's north coast.

▼ King Edward Point, where we shared drinks and tales of adventure with Paula and BAS scientists.

◀ A replica of Shackleton's small boat, and the minimalist gear for his famous traverse.

▼ Paying our respects to the great man.

This was an incredible experience for several reasons, not least the weather, which from time to time could only be described as vicious. Ocean Harbour was sheltered, or at least calm, with an intriguing grass-covered three-masted wreck on its southern side; Gold Harbour was not. In fact, we were sitting quietly down below when suddenly Steve and Al shot out of the saloon. A 70-knot gust had picked up the anchor and we were shooting backwards. They put the motor on and relaid the anchor, and all was well. This happened more than once as we wended our way south and it was not until we put our two anchors in series – the two anchors one behind the other, connected by chain before the riser chain from the second anchor to the boat – that we had no further trouble. We had already encountered huge winds crossing Royal Bay to get to Gold Harbour. I once wrote an article entitled 'South Georgia – the windiest place on Earth?' At least, it was for us.

But what compensations! All around were those attractive snow-covered mountains, a few still waiting to be climbed, and the glaciers coming down to the sea. Some of these were sublime and could be used for ski touring, which we did; some were just plain horrible, broken pitted walls of ice falling into the sea. All were intriguing. And then there was the wildlife, almost beyond description. The only colony of Weddell seals in South Georgia at Larsen, our most southerly and calmest of anchorages, with a newly born cub feeding from its mother; colonies of huge elephant seals, giant petrels, adult and newly hatched albatrosses, and of course penguins. Thousands and thousands of penguins at

St. Andrews Bay, with the youngsters a huge brown smudge corralled in the centre and surrounded by the adults for safety and security. By contrast were the leopard seals, who resented our presence, one insisting on following the dinghy from boat to shore to see us off his territory.

Three of the crew did the Shackleton traverse, one of the main reasons for the trip. I, being somewhat older and thus slower, would have required longer to do it so had to withdraw, as we were just not going to get a sufficiently long weather window. They did it in two and a half days in difficult conditions – lucky I did not go! And the passage back to the Falklands was something else again. Strong winds on the nose all the way, tacking back and forth, never being able to lay the course, heaving-to for 44 hours to ride out a storm, which we did comfortably with a Jordan Series Drogue laid out astern. We arrived at Port Stanley ten days and 400 extra nautical miles later, only just in time to catch our rearranged flights. Quite a trip, but one we would not have missed for the world.

▲◀ The first night's camp by the Trident Mountain on the Shackleton traverse.

▲▶ Negotiating a gap to get from one glacier to another on Shackleton traverse.

▶ Two and a half kilometres of tundra and terminal moraine from the glacier to the boat at their finish.

◀◀ Ski-touring on the Salomon glacier. Stuff sacks used as sledges.

Larsen, our furthest
southern anchorage and a
beautiful point to turn north.

Anchored in beautiful Wirik Bay,
South Georgia

Appendix

ANTARCTIC
REGULATIONS

ANTARCTIC REGULATIONS

Further information regarding Antarctic Regulations, kindly supplied by Barry Kennedy after recent visits (2019).

Approval for Antarctic permits are issued by the applicant's home country if the applicant is a citizen of a country that is a signatory to the Antarctic Treaty. Approval indicates that the applicant is aware of, and has made provisions to comply with, the environmental protocol of the treaty (food waste, solid waste, accidental releases). Citizens of a country that is not a signatory to the treaty are not required to seek approval to visit Antarctica.

The approval process is a pathway to research and to gain an understanding of the treaty and the treaty environmental protocol. It is used as a gauge to determine that the applicant has put thought into possible scenarios such as autonomy, vessel preparation, SAR and environmental considerations.

IAATO guidelines are not required for yachts, but are considered to represent the 'best practices' for wildlife viewing, shore landings and general operating in Antarctica. Referencing these in an application is viewed favourably by issuing authorities.

◀◀ Elephant seals and
Novara in Wirik Bay,
South Georgia.

Useful references

Contact information for permitting authorities for member nations can be found on the IAATO web page or the treaty secretariat page.

- IAATO: www.iaato.org
- Secretariat of the AntarcticTreaty: www.ats.aq/

Reference to the following sources and documents was used during the research/planning and familiarising of guidelines, policy and law governing visits to Antarctica:

- Yachting guidelines for Antarctic cruises (ATCM37)
- Antarctic-Yachting-Guideline-2016 (UK)
- Yachting Checklist (ATCM35)
- Guidelines for Environmental Impact Assessment in Antarctica
- Madrid Protocol: Annexes III and IV pertaining to treatment/ handling of waste and prevention of marine pollution in Antarctic waters
- Guidelines on Contingency Planning, Insurance, and Other Matters for Tourist and Other Non-Governmental Activities in the Antarctic Treaty Area
- Antarctic Peninsula Compendium, 3rd edition (Oceanites)
- *Southern Ocean Cruising*, 2nd Ed., Sally and Jerome Poncet
- The Protocol on Environmental Protection to the Antarctic Treaty and its Annexes
- Site Guidelines for Visitors – Antarctic Treaty Secretariat
- Plans for the Antarctic Specially Protected Areas (ASPA) and Antarctic Specially Managed Areas (ASMA)
- Wildlife Watching Guidelines (IAATO)
- General Information for Wildlife Watching (2016)
- Cetacean Watching Guidelines (2016)
- Seal Watching Guidelines (2016)
- Bird Watching Guidelines (2016)
- Non-Native Species Manual (ATCM34)
- Visitor Guidelines, IAATO
- Antarctic Conservation Act (ACA)
- www.iaato.org

▶▶ Sailing and skiing in arctic conditions may be hard work, but they're also highly rewarding.

Prehistoric musk oxen still
stand guard today.

FURTHER READING

A proper boat has to have a good library, not just for gaining knowledge, but also for inspiration. Here are some books from which we have learnt a lot.

Antarctic Oasis: Under the Spell of South Georgia, Tim and Pauline Carr (W. W. Norton, 1998)

Island at the Edge of the World: A South Georgia Odyssey, Stephen Venables (Hodder & Stoughton, 2010)

Mountaineering in Antarctica: Climbing in the Frozen South, Damien Gildea (Nevicata, 2010)

The Island Of South Georgia, Robert Headland (Cambridge University Press, 1984)

The Totorore Voyage: An Antarctic Adventure, Gerry Clark (Ebury Press, 1988)

■ INSPIRATION AND WISDOM

Addicted to Adventure: Between Rocks and Cold Places, Bob Shepton (Adlard Coles Nautical, 2014)

Endless Sea: Alone Around Antarctica – as Far South as a Boat Can Sail, Amyr Klink (Sheridan House, 2008)

High Latitude, North Atlantic: 30,000 Miles Through Cold Seas and History, John R. Bockstoce (Mystic Seaport Museum, 2003)

Into the Light: A Family's Epic Journey, Dave and Jaja Martin (Beowulf Publishing, 2002)

Mariner's Weather Handbook, Steve and Linda Dashew (Beowulf, 1998)

Mingming & the Art of Minimal Ocean Sailing, Roger D. Taylor (Fitzroy Press, 2010)

North to the Night: A Spiritual Odyssey in the Arctic, Alvah Simon (Crown Publishing, 1999)

Northern Light: One Couple's Epic Voyage from the Arctic to the Antarctic, Rolf Bjelke and Deborah Shapiro (Crown Publishing, 1986)

One Island, One Ocean: Around the Americas Aboard Ocean Watch, Herb McCormick (Weldon Owen, 2011)

Sailing Alone Around the World, Captain Joshua Slocum (Adlard Coles Nautical, 2000)

The Eight Sailing/Mountain-Exploration Books, H. W. Tilman (Mountaineers Book, 1987 – strongly recommended)

The Tototore Voyage: An Antarctic Adventure, Gerry Clark (Ebury Press, 1988)

Time on Ice: A Winter Voyage to Antarctica, Deborah Shapiro and Rolf Bjelke (International Marine/Ragged Mountain Press, 1997)

Vildmarkshav, Rolf Bjelke and Deborah Shapiro (Norstedts Förlag, 2011)

GUIDES

Admiralty Sailing Directions: Arctic Pilot Volume 3 (UK Hydrographic Office, 8th ed., 2007)

Arctic and Northern Waters, Andrew Wilkes (RCC and Imray, revised edition, 2016)

Chile: Arica Desert to Tierra Del Fuego, Andrew O'Grady (RCC and Imray, revised edition, 2017)

Norway, Judy Lomax (RCC and Imray, 2016)

Patagonia and Tierra Del Fuego Nautical Guide, Mariolina Rolfo and Giorgio Ardrizzi (English translation 3rd ed., 2015)

Sail to Svalbard, Jon Amtrup (Skagerrak Förlag, 2011)

Southern Ocean Cruising, Sally and Jérôme Poncet (Environmental Research and Assessment, 2007)

World Voyage Planner: Planning a Voyage from Anywhere in the World to Anywhere in the World, Jimmy Cornell (Adlard Coles Nautical, revised edition, 2018)

There are some useful cruising guides to South Georgia, Antarctica and Tierra del Fuego available, for free download, at the RCC website: www.rccpf.org.uk

Cape Horn and Antarctic Waters, Paul Heiney (RCC and Imray, 2017)

Den Norske Los, Svalbard og Jan Mayen, Norges Sjøkartverk

Falkland Islands Shores, Ewen Southby-Tailyour (ISBN 0-84177-341-9 and RCC supplement)

South Georgia Guide, Andrew O'Grady and Ulla Norlander (RCC)

Svalbard Guide, Pål Hermansen (Gaidaros Förlag)

The Atlantic Crossing Guide, Jane Russell (RCC, revised edition, 2017)

RESOURCES

www.explorenorth.no – company that offers high latitude consultancy, deliveries, Ski & Sail in Norway and other sail-related services. Run by the author of this book, Jon Amtrup.

www.bobshepton.co.uk – the co-author, offers delivery, skippering and consultancy services in high latitudes.

www.morganscloud.com – here you will find highly experienced sailors, engineers, boat builders, high latitude sailors and others willing to share knowledge and inspiration.

INDEX

PICTURE CREDITS